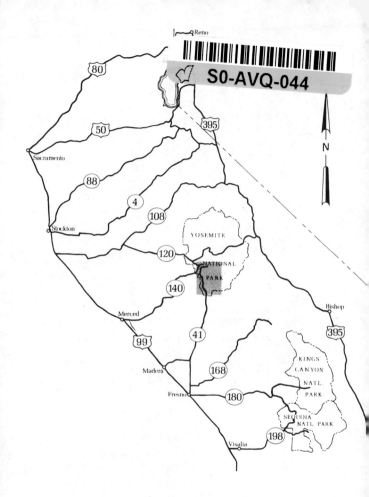

Location of the YOSEMITE quadrangle

HIGH SIERRA HIKING GUIDE

YOSEMITE

The Valley and
Surrounding Uplands

Jeffrey P. Schaffer

WILDERNESS PRESS
BERKELEY

Acknowledgments I would like to thank Ron Mackie, Jr., Yosemite's Chief Backcountry Ranger, for reviewing the fourth-edition manuscript. Almost all of this book is a condensed version of part of my Yosemite National Park guidebook, and in the "Acknowledgments" of that book I list additional people who aided me on that project.

FIFTH EDITION May 1996

Photographs, maps and design by the author
Topographic maps revised and updated by the author,
    based on U.S. Geological Survey maps
Library of Congress Card Catalog Number 96–3216
International Standard Book Number 0–89997–198–9
Manufactured in the United States of America
Published by Wilderness Press
              2440 Bancroft Way
              Berkeley, CA 94704
              (510) 843-8080

              Write for free catalog

Library of Congress Cataloging-in-Publication Data

Schaffer, Jeffrey P.
    Yosemite : a complete guide to the valley and surrounding uplands,
  including descriptions of more than 150 miles of trails / Jeffrey P.
  Schaffer. — 5th ed.
      p.   cm. — (High Sierra hiking guide)
    Includes bibliographical references (p.   ) and index.
    ISBN 0–89997–198–9
    1. Hiking—California—Yosemite National Park—Guidebooks.
  2. Trails—California—Yosemite National Park—Guidebooks.
  3. Natural history— California—Yosemite National Park—Guidebooks.
  4. Yosemite National Park (Calif.)—Guidebooks.   I. Title.
  II. Series.
  GV199.42.C22Y6772   1996
  917.94'47045—dc20   96–3216

Opposite Title Page: **Lower Yosemite Fall**

Contents

Introduction

THE WILDERNESS PRESS HIGH SIERRA HIKING GUIDES are pocket-size guides to the more popular parts of the Sierra Nevada proper. Each guide covers at least one 15-minute U.S. Geological Survey quadrangle, which is an area about 14 miles east-west by 17 miles north-south. The first page inside the front cover shows the location of the quadrangle covered by this *Yosemite* guide. Park guides adjacent to this one are *Hetch Hetchy* and *Tuolumne Meadows*.

In planning this series the editors used the 15-minute quadrangle as the unit because—though every way of dividing the Sierra is arbitrary—the quadrangle map is the chosen aid of almost every wilderness traveler. Inside the back cover is the author's updated topographic map of the quadrangle, which very accurately depicts the area's trails. With this map you can always get where you want to go, with a minimum of detours or wasted effort. (Additional map copies can be bought from Wilderness Press or its dealers. You can also buy an excellent map of Yosemite Valley published by Wilderness Press at a scale of 1:24,000.)

About two thirds of the trail descriptions in this hiking guide deal with trails in and about Yosemite Valley. Called "The Incomparable Valley," this is a magnet that attracts visitors from all over the world. As John Muir noted in the 1870s, the Sierra has several "Yosemites," though none of them matches Yosemite Valley in grandeur. Hetch Hetchy, to the north, is the foremost example of such a "Yosemite." Though some of these "Yosemites" rival or exceed Yosemite Valley in their depth or the steepness of their walls, none has the prize-winning combination of its wide, spacious floor, its world-famous waterfalls, and its unforgettable monoliths—El Capitan and Half Dome.

The rest of the trail descriptions deal with trails in a rather undramatic part of the range. However, these descriptions do include a network of trails through a grove of giant sequoias; no such trail system exists at the Park's two other groves. Although thousands of persons visit this area's Mariposa Grove each day during

Left: Yosemite Valley, viewed from Eagle Peak (Day Hike 11)

the summer, the vast majority ride the trams. The few who explore the grove on foot are richly rewarded.

One very serious drawback to visiting this guidebook's area is that its lodges, hotels and campgrounds cannot adequately handle the millions of annual visitors. Therefore, try to make reservations well in advance. The Valley's lodging plus the Wawona Hotel are operated by Yosemite Concession Services (209-252-4848). On private land in the Wawona area are The Redwoods (209-375-6256) and Camp Chilnualna (209-375-6295), which offer "cottages" with up to four bedrooms. Just outside the Park, near the start of the Glacier Point Road, is Yosemite West (209-642-2211), which offers condos and cottages. To camp in Yosemite Valley, make reservations with Destinet (1-800-436-7275). Campsites at our area's other campgrounds—Bridalveil and Wawona—are on a first-come, first-served basis. Finally, just below the Park's southern border is the USFS Summerdale Campground. South of it the Highway 41 towns of Fish Camp and Oakhurst offer additional lodging.

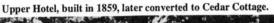

Upper Hotel, built in 1859, later converted to Cedar Cottage.

The History

"THE GRANDEUR OF THE scene was but softened by the haze that hung over the valley—light as gossamer—and by the clouds which partially dimmed the higher cliffs and mountains. This obscurity of vision but increased the awe with which I beheld it, and as I looked, a peculiar exalted sensation seemed to fill my whole being, and I found my eyes in tears with emotion." So wrote Dr. Lafayette Bunnell, a member of the Mariposa Battalion, of his group's discovery of Yosemite Valley on March 27, 1851. Today, many visitors seeing the Valley for the first time are struck with similar emotions.

The battalion entered the Valley in pursuit of a band of Ahwahnechee Indians under the leadership of Chief Teneiya. The band was captured, later released, and then decimated in 1853 by a band of Mono Indians. The Valley was now safe for tourists. James Hutchings was one of the earliest ones, and through his *Illustrated California Magazine* and his guidebooks the Valley became widely known. Roads, trails and hotels were built, guidebooks were written, and tourism increased. One important tourist was Frederick Law Olmsted, who visited the Valley and the Mariposa Grove of Big Trees in 1863 and noted that both were being ruined by commercial interests. He convinced U.S. Senator John Conness of California to introduce a park bill, which was subsequently signed by President Abraham Lincoln on June 30, 1864. The bill deeded the Valley and the Grove to California "for public use, resort and recreation."

But the lands surrounding these two tracts didn't fare well. Meadows were overgrazed by sheep (and to a lesser extent by cattle), and forests were ravaged by loggers. This habitat destruction was noted by a young Scotsman, John Muir, who first visited Yosemite Valley in 1868. Over the years he explored much of the High Sierra and criticized its exploitation, but his protestations fell on deaf ears until 1889, when he met Robert Underwood Johnson. This editor of the very influential *Century Magazine* was impressed with both Muir and the High Sierra, and he had Muir write some Yosemite articles for his magazine. A park bill was introduced in

Congress, and in October 1890, Yosemite National Park was created.

The bill, however, failed to stipulate how the Park should be administered. This task was given to the Army's Fourth Cavalry, which was stationed in Wawona. They stayed until the passage of the National Park Act of 1916, which established an administrative system for all the country's national parks and monuments. When the cavalry left Yosemite, they left behind an impressive record. They had driven sheep and cattle from the Park, had helped to settle property disputes, had laid the foundation for today's trail system, had mapped the Park in substantial detail, and had even planted trout in the Park's lakes. For Yosemite, the cavalry had by and large "come to the rescue."

One serious incursion the cavalry was unable to prevent was the creation of Hetch Hetchy Reservoir, which lies about 15 miles northwest of Yosemite Valley. John Muir and his fledgling Sierra Club had fought a losing battle to defeat this San Francisco water project. To build a massive dam required lots of timber scaffolding, and 6+ million board feet of timber were logged *inside the Park* by the Yosemite Lumber Company. More than ½ *billion* board feet of prime forest, including some of the Sierra's finest stands of sugar pines, were cut before 1930, when John D. Rockefeller, Jr. and the U.S. Government split the cost of buying up the logging company's interests. Today hikers can view part of the logged land—and walk along the abandoned railroad tracks—on Backpack Hike 2.

After World War II the Park's use greatly increased, and most of that use was confined to a small part of the Park—Yosemite Valley. The Valley was being loved to death. Beginning in 1970, the Park Service took steps to reduce the human impact in the Valley by instigating a shuttle-bus system, by reducing the number of campers and lodgers, by moving facilities and personnel outside the Valley, and by building bicycle paths. The decades-long goal of completely banning private vehicles from the Valley will never be attained until suitable camping/lodging/parking areas are developed outside the Valley, perhaps on adjacent Forest Service lands.

The Geology

NO OTHER LOCALE IN the Sierra Nevada receives so much use as does Yosemite Valley, this hiking guide's prime attraction. This has caused tremendous crowding, which in turn has led to ongoing controversy over solutions to reduce it. Likewise, the geomorphic history of the Valley—how it came to be formed—has been steeped in controversy. It began with Josiah D. Whitney, the first director of California's State Geological Survey, who proclaimed in 1865 that Yosemite Valley had been formed by down-faulting, which "explained" the angularity and verticality of its walls. Starting in 1869, John Muir explored the Yosemite area, and after several years of Sierran glacial explorations he wrote seven "Studies in the Sierra." Not only had glaciers *entirely* carved every canyon in the range, he trumpeted, but they had advanced west to the Pacific Ocean.

Not surprisingly, geologists did not accept all his findings, although over time they gravitated toward a combination of stream erosion and glacial erosion, rather than down-faulting, to explain the Valley's origin. Ironically, only James Hutchings came close to understanding how the Valley had been formed. Having lived in the Valley long enough to observe processes in action, he stood alone in recognizing the importance of mass wasting, stream erosion, flooding and former glacial erosion. He was more correct than was any geologist who followed him, but he lacked the academic credentials to be taken seriously by geologists.

To settle the Valley's origin "for all time," the U.S. Geological Survey in 1913 assigned François Matthes (pronounced "Mat'-tees") the task of explaining Yosemite Valley. All his findings would be accepted as the "Bible truth," and when his Professional Paper 160 finally appeared in 1930, it was heralded as a classic. Matthes' methodology for determining the amount of glacial erosion then was applied to glaciated ranges around the world. Unfortunately, until I began a serious investigation in the 1990s, no one had realized that his work was a fabrication. His diary indicates that he was torn between pleasing his professor, who incorrectly explained how glaciers transform landscapes, and the actual, contradictory field evidence. Ultimately, Matthes chose loyalty, wrote logical arguments, and precisely mapped glacial deposits that existed *only* in his mind. One easily visited area of his myriad deposits lies along the Four Mile Trail (Day Hike 17) at about elevation 5,150 feet. He mapped young morainal material below this elevation and old morainal material above it—but *only* bedrock and talus exist.

One reason why Matthes' work and its slight amendments by Wahrhaftig and Huber have appeared so reasonable is that most experts have thought that major uplift of the range occurred mostly during the last few million years. If this view were correct, then erosion by both rivers and glaciers must have gone on at enormous rates to create such deep canyons in so short a geologic time. Exactly when this myth of "late Cenozoic uplift" originated is unknown to the author, but it would have been reinforced by the 1872 Owens Valley earthquake near Lone Pine, which created a 23-foot-high scarp. Everyone assumed that the range rose by this amount; no one asked if Owens Valley had subsided. Yet its bedrock floor, which lies beneath thousands of feet of sediments, is in places *below* sea level. It got below sea level not through river erosion but through down-faulting.

In 1898 the uplift myth received official sanction with the USGS publication of Leslie Ransome's Bulletin 89, which used a large lava flow, standing high above the floor of the Stanislaus River canyon, to quantify uplift. Ransome assumed that the lava had flowed down the granitic bedrock floor of a *shallow, low-elevation* canyon and in response to uplift the river cut down to its current level, creating a much deeper canyon. However, most of the 9-million-year-old lava flow lies atop earlier volcanic deposits, not atop granitic bedrock. In the vicinity of the Dardanelles, the base of the lava flow is a full 1,200 feet above a rhyolite deposit that is at least 23 million years old. Therefore, the canyon was *at least* 1,200 feet deeper than Ransome had believed—perhaps much deeper, since most of the earliest deposits have been eroded away. Ironically, Ransome had mapped the volcanic deposits correctly; he merely ignored the lower, older deposits that contradicted his uplift hypothesis. Huber did the same in 1981 for the San Joaquin River drainage and in 1990 for the Tuolumne River drainage.

Fortunately, there are dozens of dated, mostly volcanic, deposits

Tenaya Canyon and Half Dome, viewed from Glacier Point

in the Sierra Nevada, and their bases are in contact with the topography they buried. Therefore, one can recreate that former topography and see how it compares with today's topography. By doing this in my Ph.D. dissertation (see Recommended Reading), I was able to show that over the last 15 million years of essentially modern climate, during which time almost all Sierran uplift supposedly has occurred, resistant ridges and monoliths have been reduced only by about five feet! Canyon bottoms have been eroded more: perhaps tens of feet, certainly not thousands of feet. For example, the net erosion over the last *50 million years* in the South Yuba River canyon near Malakoff Diggins is too minor to measure. And some 20 million years ago the Clark Fork Stanislaus River, like others, was buried under voluminous deposits. Fortunately, some still remain near the headwaters. What they show is that the granitic landscape back then was virtually identical to today's, including all the glacial landforms—cirques, hanging tributaries, etc.—that supposedly have been created over the last 2 million years of major, episodic glaciation. Additionally, these deep, old canyons contradict the uplift myth: had major uplift occurred, then the canyon floors initially would have been thousands of feet *below* sea level.

So where does this leave us with Yosemite Valley? The granitic rocks in which it has developed solidified as discrete bodies—plutons—beneath the earth's surface from 114 to 86 million years ago. Through intense weathering and erosion characteristic of tropical climates, much of the Valley's granitic rocks could have been exposed by 75 million years ago. Most of the Sierra's plutons would have been exposed by then. Consequently, at the onset of uplift the Sierra's rivers already were entrenched in granitic canyons at middle elevations and entrenched in granitic and/or metamorphic canyons at lower elevations, as they are today. From about 75 to about 33 million years ago, *tropical* weathering and erosional processes continued to modify the Valley, which took on a steep-walled, broad-floored aspect early on.

By the advent of modern climates 33 million years ago, you would have recognized the Valley. It would have been close to its present depth and about three-fourths its present width. Immediately before the first glaciation, about 2 million years ago, the Valley looked very much as it does today. Minor widening occurred through retreat parallel to existing surfaces, not to steepening of slopes. The Valley back then still would have been the rock climbers' Mecca of the world. My estimate of *average* wall retreat during this time is less than 500 feet, most of it due to rockfall rather than to glacial erosion. However, retreat of thick glaciers reduced pressure against the lower slopes, and this pressure release apparently induced rockfall, so glaciers *indirectly* widened Yosemite Valley, albeit minimally, despite glaciers entering the Valley perhaps up to four dozen times. The earliest glaciers excavated up to 2,000 feet of fractured, tropically weathered bedrock lying beneath the Valley's broad floor, replacing it over time with glacial and stream sediments. The last glacier entered about 35,000 years ago, advanced through the Valley and into the Merced Gorge, then began to retreat about 16,000 years ago, leaving the Valley about 14,000 years ago. Supposedly the Valley then was occupied by a deep lake—another geomyth, dating back at least to Whitney. This guide's trail descriptions have elaborations on this brief discourse, and they identify evidence you can examine for yourself.

The Biology

YOU CANNOT FORGET your first visit to Yosemite: the enormous granite monoliths of El Capitan, the Cathedral Rocks and Half Dome, the leaping, tumultuous waterfalls, the glacially smoothed domes of Tuolumne Meadows, the pristine lakes and snow-clad high peaks. Of these features only the waterfalls move, and none are living. For most visitors, memories of living forms—except for giant sequoias—are likely to take a back seat to the inanimate landscape, although many out-of-state visitors will be duly impressed with the size of some conifers besides the sequoias. But despite the seemingly barren summits and cliffs, Yosemite is predominantly a landscape of forest green. Along most of this guide's trails, conifers shade our way.

The largest conifer in our area is the giant sequoia, which is the uncontested holder of the world heavyweight crown. Its ancestors go back to the days of the dinosaurs, but we don't know where it originated or when it migrated westward into the Sierra Nevada. The trees of the southern Sierra would have entered it no later than about 33 million years ago, if not by before 65 million years ago. Those of the northern Sierra would have entered it no later than about 15 million years ago.

The tree's size hasn't always assured it success. It is adapted to gentle-to-moderate slopes possessing sufficient soil moisture to endure the dry summers. Its seeds are not eaten and transported by migrating birds, hence some suitable slopes are not colonized. Also, for its seeds to produce viable seedlings, the tree needs cone-boring cerambycid beetles, seed-eating Douglas' squirrels (chickarees), and periodic fires. Remove any of these, and a sequoia grove is in peril. (For more sequoia natural history, see **Day Hike 25**).

Fire, which is essential for sequoias, also is important for many sun-loving plants—and the animals that depend on them. In this guide's area, much of the forest has been burned since a major fire in 1974. After a forest fire, wildflowers and shrubs greatly increase their numbers. Over time, they may be succeeded by oaks, which shade them out at lower elevations, while pines and incense-cedars do so higher up. Possibly firs may come to dominate the forest, if abundant soil moisture is present. If fires occur fairly regularly—

Top left: cones of ponderosa pine (top), Douglas-fir (right) and sugar pine (bottom). Top right: cones of western white pine (left) and red fir (right). Bottom: white-fir branches (left) versus red-fir branches (right).

every decade or two—litter accumulation will be minor and only ground fires will result, eliminating brush and young trees. If fires do not occur for many decades, litter accumulation will be major and a crown fire will result, destroying a forest and allowing the process of plant succession to begin once again.

A sequoia grove is a relatively restricted plant community, which, like our area's other plant communities, includes animals and microorganisms as well as plants. As in that community, the plants, animals, and microorganisms in other communities are regulated in number largely by their mutual interactions and by nonbiotic influences such as soil, slope, and microclimate. If you drive from Arch Rock Entrance Station up to Yosemite Valley and then up the Glacier Point Road to the Mono Meadow trailhead (**Backpack Hike 4**), you'll pass through several plant communities.

From the entrance station you'll drive mostly through a canyon live (gold-cup) oak woodland, although shrubs such as Mariposa manzanitas dominate dry spots, as at the foot of El Capitan. Walking through the woodland, you'll find it seemingly devoid of animals, save perhaps for raucous Steller's jays or acorn and pileated woodpeckers. But the animals are there. The oak's roots are tapped by root fungi, which are grazed by flat bugs and carrion beetles, which are eaten by western skinks (lizards), which are preyed upon by gopher snakes, which are seized by mountain king snakes, which are carried off by red-tailed hawks. And there are hundreds more interacting species. Incidentally, among this vegetation, where ground rodents abound, so do rattlesnakes.

As you drive on toward Bridalveil Fall, you'll pass through a mixed-conifer forest, dominated by ponderosa pine, incense-cedar (not a true cedar), white fir, and Douglas-fir (not a true fir). Black oaks have replaced live oaks and, correspondingly, western gray squirrels have replaced California ground squirrels.

The shady forest is a stark contrast to Yosemite Valley's meadows, which, like the large one at Wawona, have been greatly altered from their natural state. Early Valley residents lowered the water table to drain bogs, which led to meadow invasion by trees. Introduced livestock grazed heavily on the native meadow plants, though these plants were most affected by the usually unintentional introduction of alien plants. Galen Clark noted that in the 30 years that had passed since the Valley had been given "protection," its luxuriant native grasses and wildflowers had decreased to only one-fourth of their original number.

From the Valley you'll drive west up to lower, open slopes of Turtleback Dome, then head south up to a junction with the Glacier Point Road. Along this leg are local areas of dense shrubs—mostly ceanothus—as well as forest areas that have sugar pines, which were extensively logged before 1930.

On the Glacier Point Road you'll climb east, entering a red-fir forest before arriving at Badger Pass. This is replaced by a lodge-pole-pine forest in the flatlands of the Bridalveil Campground area. This rather sudden change in tree type is due to the flat's high water tables; the lodgepoles embrace it, the red firs abhor it.

Where the road bends north, you'll reach the Mono Meadow Trail, which begins in a grove of mature red firs. The forest floor is very shady, so few plants grow on it. Some that do, such as the snow plant, derive part of their nourishment by tapping their roots into soil fungi. The forest has a solemn, cathedral-like feeling, for the trees are lofty and silence usually prevails. With little plant life on the forest floor, there is an absence of scolding rodents and singing birds.

If you were to take the Mono Meadow Trail east to the Buena Vista Trail and follow it south, you'd climb into other communities. With elevation you'd note western white ("silver") pines, followed by snow-loving mountain hemlocks. The hemlocks, unfortunately, prolong the duration of snow cover, which is a nuisance to hikers but a boon to snow mosquitoes. These blood-suckers (the females, that is) may be annoying to you, but they are major pollinators of the area's wildflowers.

The Buena Vista Trail guides you to the Buena Vista Peak environs, which lie in the subalpine realm. Many plants up there are dwarfed, for winter's driving, subfreezing winds are extreme, and plants survive better buried under snow than protruding above it. Near the top of 9,709-foot Buena Vista Peak—the highest summit in our area—stunted, gnarled whitebark pines grow in dense clusters. These attract Clark's nutcrackers, which are large, gray relatives of jays. The birds thrive on the pines' seeds, and they bury caches to last them through the year. The birds will eat most of the seeds, but a few survive to give rise to more pines. Thus the birds help to perpetuate the clusters of whitebark pines, just as the Douglas' squirrels, lower down, help to perpetuate the groves of giant sequoias.

The Trails

THIS GUIDEBOOK IS AIMED at hikers—day hikers in particular. The eastern half of Yosemite Valley also has bike paths, which are mentioned where encountered or used in this guide. Bicyclists share these with hikers, but horses are banned—a definite plus for those eschewing horse manure and urine. Seasonally (during the summer and then some), both horses and bikes can be rented.

The hikes in this book are two kinds: day hikes and backpack hikes. For the latter, you'll need a wilderness permit, which you can get in person either at the Yosemite Valley Wilderness Center, located near the Valley's Visitor Center, or at the Wawona Ranger Station. Unfortunately, backcountry overuse has made a quota system necessary. Up to fifty percent of each trailhead quota may be reserved in advance by mail, phone, or in person at the Wilderness Center (write to Wilderness Reservations, Wilderness Center, P.O. Box 545, Yosemite, CA 95389, or phone at 209-372-0740). The following information is needed to process your reservation: name, address, phone number, number of people and stock (no pets!) in your party, entry and exit dates, starting and ending trailheads, principal destination, and all alternative trailheads and dates you are willing to accept. In the mid-1990s the center charged $3.00 *per person*. If you don't reserve in advance but rather apply in person, the wilderness permit is free.

There are three advantages to day hiking. First, you don't have to worry about the wilderness-permit hassle. Second, you don't have to worry about protecting your food overnight in backcountry bearproof boxes, or in bulky, heavy, bear-resistant food canisters (which you can rent), or in food sacks bearbagged on horizontal cables or tree limbs. Bears, incidentally, rarely molest hikers; mostly they, like rodents, go after your food. Finally, you don't need to boil, filter, or chemically treat pristine-looking but possibly polluted backcountry water, for you can carry a day's supply of water in your pack. Before hiking, familiarize yourself with advice, cautions, and regulations found in the quarterly newspaper, the *Yosemite Guide,* available at every entrance station.

Note that each hike in this book has a grade: a number-letter combination. The numbers refer to each hike's *total* mileage, as follows: **1**=0–4.9 miles, **2**=5.0–9.9 miles, **3**=10.0–14.9 miles, **4**=15.0–19.9 miles, and **5**=20.0+ miles. The letters refer to your *total* elevation gain: **A**=0–499 feet, **B**=500–999 feet, **C**=1,000–1,999 feet, **D**=2,000–3,999 feet, and **E**=4,000+ feet. The words *easy, moderate,* and *strenuous* describe a hike's difficulty for a person in *good* shape, given the recommended time. Of course, you can decrease the difficulty of most hikes by taking longer to do them.

At the end of each trailhead description is a **boldfaced** letter-number combination, which corresponds to the letter-number grid on the book's map where the hike starts. This is provided for those hikers not familiar with the trail system of this part of the Park.

In a year of normal precipitation, the trails are virtually snow-free from early July through early October, although down in Yosemite Valley and about Wawona, they are free from about early April through late November. When your trail is partly snowbound, you can usually still follow it with the aid of ducks or blazes. A duck is made up of two or more rocks, arranged in an obviously unnatural fashion. Ducks are often placed along a trail where it traverses bedrock. A blaze is a scar hewn in a trailside tree trunk, usually in the shape of an **i** or a **T**.

To see wildflowers at their prime (also prime mosquito time), visit the lower trails in May or June and the higher ones in July. If you plan to swim in a backcountry lake, in the Valley's Merced River, or in Wawona's South Fork Merced River, visit in late July or early August, when water temperature usually is at its maximum. Wawona's South Fork can be quite warm by mid-afternoon.

Of course, many people visit Yosemite to see its waterfalls, which usually are best from mid-May to mid-June. Avoid, however, the Memorial Day weekend—and the Fourth of July and Labor Day weekends—when the Park becomes severely overcrowded. For relative solitude, visit the Valley or Wawona from mid-September through November, when the summer crowds are gone and the skiers have not yet arrived.

Day Hike 1
Valley Floor, West Loop

Distance: 6.9 miles (11.1 km) loop trip

Grade: 2B, easy half-day hike

Trailhead: Bridalveil Fall parking lot, 120 yards before the descending Wawona Road reaches a junction on the floor of Yosemite Valley. **C1.**

Introduction: This is the first of six Yosemite Valley floor hikes in this book, which are arranged from west to east. On this first loop hike you'll see Bridalveil Fall, the Cathedral Rocks, and El Capitan all at close range.

Description: You could start this loop from any of several pullouts along the Valley's roads, but we're starting from the Bridalveil Fall Parking lot, since it has the most parking space. From the lot's east end you hike just two minutes on a paved trail to a junction, veer right and parallel a Bridalveil Creek tributary as you climb an equally short trail up to its end. During May and June, when Bridalveil Fall is at its best, your trail's-end viewpoint will be drenched in spray, making the last part of the trail very slippery and making photography from this vantage point nearly impossible. Early settlers named this fall for its filmy, veil-like aspect, which it has in summer after its flow has greatly diminished. However, their predecessors, the Miwok Indians, named it *Pohono,* the "fall of the puffing winds," for at low volume its water is pushed around by gusts of wind.

After descending back to the trail junction and turning right, we quickly encounter three branches of Bridalveil Creek, each churning along a course that cuts through old rockfall debris. From a junction with a short trail to the Valley's eastbound road, we continue ahead on our broad trail—the old Wawona Road until 1933—and almost reach the present road, then quickly veer right to climb up to the crest of Bridalveil Moraine. From it we get a good view of the loose west wall of Lower Cathedral Rock and also of overhanging Leaning Tower.

Bridalveil Fall or *Pohono,* the fall of the puffing winds

Just past the moraine's crest we enter a gully lined with big-leaf maples, and here we have an excellent head-on view of mammoth El Capitan. Then, while only yards away from the base of the forbidding north face of Lower Cathedral Rock, we see a high, broad ledge, covered with canyon live oaks, that almost cuts the face in two. We continue east through a conifer forest, soon crossing a narrow, open, talus field. At its base stands a second moraine, similar to Bridalveil Moraine. Both were left about 14–15,000 years ago, when the last glacier, while receding, temporarily halted its retreat and dropped some of its load.

Walking among white firs, incense-cedars, ponderosa pines, Douglas-firs, and black oaks, we continue on a generally view-impaired route to a brief climb almost to the base of overwhelming Middle Cathedral Rock, and here you'll find it worth your effort to scramble 50 yards up to the actual base. Touching the base of this monolith's overpowering, 2,000-foot-high face can be a humbling experience. Next we traverse briefly beneath the massive northeast face and its two pinnacles, and then descend slightly to a level area, from which you could walk northwest a bit to a turnout on the eastbound road. From that turnout you can plainly see the Cathedral Spires. These spires, and the 500-foot-high buttress they stand on, resemble a two-towered Gothic cathedral—hence the name. Despite their apparent inaccessibility, both were first climbed way back in 1934, during the early days of Valley climbing. Now, each is harder to climb, since rockfall altered the original ascent routes.

About a ⅓-mile walk beyond the level area we arrive at a signed trail, veer left, northwest, on it, and descend to a point on the eastbound road only 20 yards west of the Cathedral Picnic Area entrance. Those few who head north to the picnic area are rewarded with two classic views, one of El Capitan and the other of the Three Brothers. Our route, however, continues northwest almost to a bend in the Merced River, from which you may see on summer days, sunbathers basking on the long, sandy beach of the far bank. Since our route eventually goes over to that vicinity, summertime hikers with swimsuits on can shortcut across the wide, chest-deep Merced to that beach. Non-swimmers follow the trail briefly west to the El Capitan Bridge. Here, by the eastern edge of El Capitan Meadow, the hiker gets reflective views of the Cathedral Rocks, and one can see why the Miwok Indians visualized the lower rock as a giant acorn.

From the El Capitan Bridge you walk north either along the road or its adjacent riverbank trail to a sharp bend. By continuing east from there for about 250 yards you reach the site of Devils Elbow Picnic Area, closed in 1993 due to riverbank erosion from heavy use. However, above a second river bend there is access to the sandy beach and its nearby mid-river rockfall boulder—perfect for diving.

From the first river bend we cross the main road and start west along an old road that in ⅓ mile comes to a small hollow from whose north end a climbers' trail ascends to the foot of El Capitan. This is a worthy excursion. The 3,000-foot route from the foot up its "Nose" takes only one day for world-class climbers, and the first to ascend it without direct-aid slings was Lynn Hill. Rock climbing is a sport where women indeed are on par with men.

Beyond the hollow our road rolls gently west and then southwest to a trail branching west. We stick to the closed road and quickly reach the Valley's westbound road at the west end of El Capitan Meadow. After the Park was created in 1890 this meadow became the Valley's first campground and Bridalveil Meadow soon became the second. Three other free, meadow campgrounds soon followed, in contrast to the forested ones today. Back then, horse pasturage was the prime concern, hence the need for meadow sites.

Leaving the meadow's edge you walk briefly west along the paved road and cross two seasonal branches of Ribbon Creek. In ¼ mile you come to a dirt road, and by walking just a few paces up it you immediately reach a westbound trail. After walking about five minutes west on it you cross a low recessional moraine, then drop almost to the paved road's edge. Here a turnout provides drivers and hikers with an unobstructed view of Bridalveil Fall.

Under the pleasant shade of ponderosa pines and incense-cedars you continue west, passing some cabin-size rockfall blocks immediately before skirting the north end of the Bridalveil Meadow moraine. Soon you enter a swampy area with cattails and at its west end cross trickling Black Spring. Past the spring your trail more or less parallels the westbound road, shortly arriving at the back side of the Valley View scenic turnout. Here you see El Capitan, Bridalveil Fall and the Cathedral Rocks magnificently rising high above the stately conifers that line Bridalveil Meadow. Barely rising above the trees are the distant landmarks of Clouds Rest, Half Dome, and Sentinel Rock.

Beyond Valley View our forested trail quickly reaches its westernmost point at Pohono Bridge. From a stream-gaging station across it our feet tread a riverside path past popular roadside Fern Spring, then past generally unknown trailside Moss Spring. Mountain (Pacific) dogwoods add springtime beauty as sunlight filters down to light up their translucent leaves and their large, petal-like, creamy-white bracts. Douglas-firs locally dominate as we hike to Bridalveil Meadow. Here we walk northeast along the eastbound road's side, staying above a seasonally boggy meadow. By the far edge the trail resumes, and goes north to a bend to cross the Bridalveil Meadow moraine. Previously this has been called the *terminal* moraine of the last glacier, but that one actually advanced about five miles farther, down into the lower part of Merced Gorge. Forty yards north of the bend is a plaque on a large rock, dedicated to Dr. Lafayette Bunnell, who was in the Valley's 1851 discovery party.

From the moraine you parallel the Merced River southeast almost to the eastbound road, which you can take 0.2 mile east to the Wawona Road, then go briefly up it to the Bridalveil Fall parking lot. Doing so in springtime avoids the possibility of getting wet feet in the nearby fords of multibranched Bridalveil Creek. After the last creek crossing the trail parallels the creek's northern branch east about 300 yards to long turnouts on both sides of the eastbound road. Here you can head southwest on the road to the parking lot or from the turnout on the far side of the road find a short trail going southeast to the trail you originally started on. On it retrace your steps 0.3 mile southwest to the lot.

Day Hike 2
Valley Floor, Yosemite Lodge Loop

Distance: 7.0 miles (11.3 km) loop trip

Grade: 2A, easy half-day hike

Trailhead: Yosemite Falls parking lot, which is just west of the Yosemite Creek bridge. If full, try parking just south, in the Yosemite Lodge. Better yet, take the shuttle bus to the lot. **D1.**

North Dome, Clouds Rest and Half Dome, from Leidig Meadow

Introduction: Most of this loop is relatively quiet and lightly traveled. On it you'll get a classic view of the Three Brothers plus other less famous but equally dramatic views.

Description: Behind the restrooms at the west end of the Yosemite Falls parking lot you'll find a trail heading southwest. On it you almost touch the main road, then curve right to the base of Swan Slab, which is a low cliff that attracts many climbers. A little less than ½ mile from the falls' lot you reach the Yosemite Falls trail (**Day Hike 10**), then pass above Sunnyside Walk-In Campground, a no-reservation campground heavily patronized by climbers. The trail next descends south along the campground's west edge, then parallels the Valley's westbound road ¼ mile before crossing it.

On another trail segment you parallel the road southwest, and in about a minute you may see a trail, branching southeast. This goes across the west edge of grassy Leidig Meadow to a sandy beach beside the Merced River, and then parallels it about ½ mile upstream to a long, sturdy, foot-and-bike bridge that spans this river. From the west edge of the meadow you get one of the Valley's best views, which includes North Dome, Royal Arches, Washington Column, Clouds Rest, and Half Dome. Partly obscuring Half Dome is a large descending ridge on whose dry slopes the Four Mile Trail (**Day Hike 17**) zigzags down from Glacier Point. Looking west from Leidig Meadow, you see the Three Brothers, named for three sons of Chief Teneiya who were taken prisoner here in May 1851 by the Mariposa Battalion. The vertical east face of Middle Brother was the origin of a March 1987 rockfall that left most of the rocky debris you are about to cross. The road here is temporarily closed by rockfall every few years.

From the trail junction the main trail quickly is sandwiched between the westbound road above and the silent river below. Light-colored, giant boulders from recent rockfalls contrast with darker, lichen-covered ones of much older rockfalls. Soon we leave the river's side and parallel the road at a short distance, hiking through a forest of pine, incense-cedar, and oak. After a mile of walking along the trail, part with fair views, we arrive at the El Capitan Picnic Area site, closed due to riverbank erosion from overuse (now no river access). A trail north-northeast goes to the westbound road and the new picnic area. In ⅓ mile we enter a meadow and have views of many of the Valley's features, particularly El Capitan, the Three Brothers, and the Cathedral Rocks. In the past our path split in the meadow, the two branches then rejoining in about 0.1 mile at the roadside site of the Devil Elbow Picnic Area, also closed due to overuse. However, there still is access to its sandy beach and a nearby mid-river rockfall boulder that is perfect for diving.

From the picnic area site our trail quickly curves south, hugging both road and fenced-off river for ¼ mile to the El Capitan Bridge—one of the Valley's most scenic spots (see **Day Hike 1**), where again there is river access. At the bridge's east end the trail resumes, heads east to a bank opposite the south end of the Devils Elbow beach, then angles southeast to the eastbound road. Just 20 yards east lies the entrance to the Cathedral Picnic Area and on its road we walk north down to the riverbank for two famous and instructive views. Look northeast and note the similarity among the Three Brothers. They present a classic case of joint-controlled topography. Each is bounded on the east and south by nearly vertical joint planes and on the west by an oblique-angle joint plane. These three planes govern the shape of each brother. Now look northwest and see the massive south face of El Capitan and on the east part of it identify the dark-gray "North America map," which is a band of diorite that intruded and then solidified within the slightly older El Capitan granite.

Leaving the willow-lined Merced, we return to our trail, cross the road, and walk 250 yards southeast to a junction with the Valley's south-side trail. On it we start east and immediately cross a creek bed that is lined with youthful ponderosa pines which sprang up after a flood. Upstream we see overhanging Taft Point, then see it again as we progress east. After ½ mile of shady, south-side walking, we come to a huge, trailside slab, on whose flat summit are about 20 mortar holes made by the Indians to grind acorns to flour. Not a glacier-transported rock, this 1,000-ton slab broke off a steep wall of the obvious side canyon above us. As we continue on, Douglas-firs and white firs mingle with the more dominant ponderosa pines, incense-cedars, and black oaks.

We have scattered views over the next mile, which takes us to Sentinel Creek—usually reduced to just a trickle by the first day of summer. After the summer solstice you're lucky if multistage Sentinel Fall, located high in the creek's canyon, is even a gossamer mist. Voluminous only in flood stage, this fall is best seen in the warming days of late May.

After crossing the creek we come to an old spur road—the end of the Four Mile Trail from Glacier Point (**Day Hike 17**). In this vicinity once stood Leidig's Hotel, the westernmost of several pioneer hotels. Beyond here our trail soon draws close to the Valley's eastbound road, and where we see a large parking area, about ¼ mile beyond the old spur road, we leave our trail, cross the eastbound road, and enter a picnic area. Black's Hotel once stood in this area, together with Galen Clark's cabin. Clark was one of the Valley's first tourists, and later became Yosemite's first guardian.

Descending through the picnic area we reach a long, sturdy bridge that replaces a much earlier suspension bridge across the Merced River. It provides good views of Yosemite Falls, Royal Arches, Washington Column, North Dome, Clouds Rest, Sentinel Rock, the Cathedral Rocks, and the Three Brothers. From its far end, a riverside path starts west to skirt Leidig Meadow. We take a broad, paved foot-and-bike path north to a bend in the road on the grounds of Yosemite Lodge. The path next winds northeast, then heads north, finally crossing the Valley's westbound road on the east side of the entrance to the lodge's grounds. This spot is also the west entrance to the Yosemite Falls parking lot, your starting point.

Day Hike 3
Valley Floor, Yosemite Village Loop

Distance: 3.3 miles (5.4 km) loop trip
Grade: 1A, easy 2-hour hike
Trailhead: Same as for Day Hike 2. **D1.**
Introduction: Famous views of Yosemite Falls, Half Dome, and Royal Arches are seen along this short hike.
Description: Avoiding hordes of visitors going north to the Lower Yosemite Fall bridge, we start from the parking lot's east end and walk southeast, quickly bridge Yosemite Creek, then cross the main road to start east on a trail along its south side. Our trail quickly branches, and we angle right, away from the road to immediately cross a short spur road south. Beyond it our paved foot-and-bike path enters a beautiful, view-packed meadow, through which we start southeast but have the option to branch right, bridge the Merced River, and head toward the Yosemite chapel.

By not branching right in the meadow, we end at a parking area with picnic tables, just north of a 1994-vintage Sentinel Bridge, built immediately above the site of its predecessor. Often during August, when Upper Yosemite Fall is only a vestige of its springtime self, rafters with life vests slowly float down the river, adding a human element to the famous tree-framed view of stately Half Dome. By strategically locating their hotel in the area between this bridge and the chapel, Buck Beardsley and G. Hite in 1859 provided guests with the best of all possible views. Business, however, was poor, and in 1864 James Hutchings—one of the Valley's first tourists—bought the hotel.

From the south end of Sentinel Bridge we walk east on a paved riverbank trail, then cross the adjacent one-way road. Now we continue east beside the road, pass the seasonally bustling Housekeeping Camp, and soon arrive at the granite-stone LeConte Memorial Lodge. It is named for Joseph LeConte, who was the first geology professor at Berkeley's then-infant University of California. During the summer of 1870 he visited Yosemite Valley, met John Muir, and was profoundly impressed by both.

Leaving the lodge, its trailside Indian mortar holes, and its large boulders chalked by climbers, we cross the road and follow a short path north along the east side of the Housekeeping Camp, reaching a bridge that links this camp to Lower Riverside Campground. Heading toward Yosemite Falls, we leave behind views of Glacier Point, Glacier Point Apron, and Grizzly Peak as we follow a path downstream alongside alders and willows. On this short stretch large blocks were laid along the bank to prevent the river from meandering into either camp. All told, the river was once lined with about 14,500 feet of rip-rap revetment. Ponderosa pines, incense-cedars, and black oaks shade us to a small stretch of Ahwahnee Meadow that we cross just before the Valley's central road. In it our foot-and-bike path crosses a dirt path and momentarily we head straight toward Upper Yosemite Fall. Here we have clear views east of North Dome, Royal Arches, Washington Column, and Half Dome. Below these towering landmarks stands one of America's grandest hotels, the Ahwahnee, opened in 1927.

After we cross the central road we walk north, shaded by large black oaks growing along the west edge of Ahwahnee Meadow. In ¼ mile we reach the west end of the Church Bowl, which has a paved roadside path, and just behind it, a dirt one, which we ascend northwest into canyon live oaks. Climbing from the Church Bowl up past the Valley's medical clinic, we quickly reach Indian Canyon Creek. Its canyon was a principal Valley exit used by the Indians heading up to the north rim, and early pioneers built a trail of sorts up to it, then west to a Yosemite Falls overlook. In early season you may note one of the Valley's lesser-known falls, Lehamite Falls, which plunges down a branch of Indian Canyon.

Beyond the canyon's creek and its huge rockfall boulders (the Valley has widened more from rockfall than from glacial erosion), we climb northwest to avoid Park buildings and residences, then contour west beneath sky-piercing Arrowhead Spire and the highly fractured Castle Cliffs. Approaching a spur trail down to nearby government stables, we spy Lost Arrow—a giant pinnacle high on the wall of Upper Yosemite Fall. Heading west ¼ mile toward

Lower Yosemite Fall, we come to a junction. From it a trail descends along Yosemite Creek to our trailhead, but we continue ¼ mile west to reach the highly visited bridge near the base of Lower Yosemite Fall. Along this last stretch a sawmill once stood, its large blade powered by the creek's water. John Muir built this sawmill for James Hutchings "to cut lumber for cottages . . . from the fallen pines which had been blown down in a violent windstorm [winter of 1867–68]."

From the bridge May and June visitors are treated to the thunderous roar and copious spray of the lower fall, but by late August the fall is usually reduced to a mist, and in some years it dries entirely by September. Dry or not, the fall should not be examined at close range, for even if boulder-choked Yosemite Creek is bonedry, its rocks are water-polished and very slippery. Before leaving the bridge, note how the lower fall has indirectly cut its alcove. Stream erosion has barely cut into the granitic bedrock since the last glacier disappeared about 14,000 years ago, but in winter the fall's spray freezes in the surrounding rocks, expands, and pries loose lower slabs that in turn remove support from the upper ones. The resulting myriad rockfall boulders then over time are rounded by stream action. These boulders, being locally derived, offer a gauge with which to estimate the amount of postglacial alcove rockfall. Walking back to your parking-lot trailhead, stop many times to get views of both Upper and Lower Yosemite Falls. Long ago a swath of trees was logged just to provide these views.

Day Hike 4
Valley Floor, Camp Curry Loop

Distance: 2.8 miles (4.5 km) loop trip
Grade: 1A, easy 2-hour hike
Trailhead: Camp Curry parking lot, in eastern Yosemite Valley. **D1.**
Introduction: More like a stroll, this is the easiest hike described in this guide. It is recommended for those who enjoy a leisurely pace, who want to take time to commune with squirrels, birds, and wild-

flowers, and who want to reflect on the Valley's natural and human history.

Description: Back in the 1860s, long before a car entered the Valley, what is now the Camp Curry parking lot was an apple orchard, and rows of these fruit trees still grow in it today. From the lot's southeast corner we follow a paved path east along the south edge of a paved road. Both soon bend southeast and equally soon reach a junction with a shuttle-bus road to Happy Isles. Seventy yards beyond the junction our path crosses a short spur road to a trailhead parking lot for *wilderness-permit holders only* (e.g., **Backpack Hike 1**). This lot was a former garbage dump, which attracted bears, which were fed by rangers until 1941—the start of the bear problem. As backpackers became far more numerous in the 1960s, "delinquent" Yosemite bears who were kicked out of the Valley pursued them into new territory and eventually over much of the High Sierra. From this lot you can also hike up to the base of broad, curving Glacier Point Apron, a good place to view climbers. "Sticky soled" shoes, developed in the 1980s, allowed climbers to waltz up new routes that would have been unthinkable in the '70s.

You could take the paved, roadside path to Happy Isles, but a quieter one begins from the southeast edge of the trailhead parking lot. This rolls southeast, staying about 100–150 yards from the unseen shuttle-bus road. In ⅓ mile it intersects a southbound stock trail that links the Valley stables to the John Muir Trail. Beyond this intersection we head east on planks across a boggy area, and although mosquitoes may be bothersome in late spring and early summer, the bog then produces its best wildflowers. At a huge, lone boulder by the bog's east side, our trail angles southeast toward the hub of the Happy Isles area.

You'll probably see dozens if not hundreds of visitors in this area, and here you'll find, besides restrooms near the shuttle-bus road, an informative nature center. Spend some time to study its exhibits and perhaps take in a show or a nature walk. Also visit the two Happy Isles, each surrounded by the splashing, joyously chorusing Merced River.

Departing north from Happy Isles, you have a choice of three pleasant routes: the Merced's west-bank trail, its east-bank trail, and the shuttle-bus road's east-side trail. The east-side trail begins about 100 yards north of a stream-gaging station, where it branches right, away from the east-bank trail. On the east-side trail you pass some cabin-size, moss-and-lichen-covered rockfall blocks, and then, where the trail climbs to cross the "Medial Moraine" (actually a recessional end moraine left by the Merced River glacier), you descend momentarily west to cross the road to the west-bending river. Both riverbank trails are relaxing strolls along the azalea-lined river, but perhaps the east-bank trail is more interesting since it traverses along the base of the west-trending moraine.

Skirting the base, the east-bank trail goes northwest almost to the Valley stables. There, at the moraine's end, turn left and immediately cross Clarks Bridge, named for Galen Clark, the Park's first guardian. From its west side, west-bank-trail hikers now join us for a brief walk past the entrances to the Upper and Lower Pines campgrounds. Beyond them we soon meet the southeast-heading shuttle-bus road, cross it, and walk west along a roadside trail leading past the north edge of our parking-lot trailhead.

Day Hike 5
Valley Floor, Mirror Lake Loop

Distance: 3.6 miles (5.9 km) loop trip

Grade: 1A, easy 2-hour hike

Trailhead: Walk or take the shuttle bus through the Pines campgrounds to a shuttle-bus stop just across Clarks Bridge, and near a parking lot for patrons of the Yosemite stables. **D1.**

Introduction: First cars and then shuttle buses once went to Mirror Lake and Indian Caves, but now the road is used by bicyclists. Most hikers also use it, though paths offer quieter route to these sites.

Description: The low ridge you see just behind the shuttle-bus stop is the Valley's "Medial Moraine," so named because early geologists thought it formed where the Tenaya Creek and Merced River glaciers merged. A trail goes east along each side of the moraine, the south-side, riverbank trail being more scenic and quieter. On it we walk east along the base of the moraine, then at a junction veer left to the adjacent shuttle-bus road. Immediately before this junction is a large white rock derived from the upper Merced River drainage, indicating that *its* receding glacier left this end moraine.

We cross the road and ascend a spur trail about 40 yards east to a main trail. Starting north on it we immediately top the moraine's crest, then descend northwest toward a road junction. The shuttle-bus road goes west to our starting point while bicyclists bound for Mirror Lake take the road north. Still on our trail, we meander north, skirting an area of giant rockfall boulders that testify to the instability of Half Dome's west flank. Beyond them we come to a trail intersection beside Tenaya Bridge. North, our trail soon reaches the Indian Caves area. West, the other trail parallels Tenaya Creek to the back side of the stables. Our route takes this other trail briefly east, then northeast ½ mile up along the creek to a footbridge.

We cross the footbridge, climb briefly to the paved bike road, and head up it past a seasonally popular swimming hole, which lies just below the outlet of Mirror Lake. (By this pond is the start of a southwest-heading foot trail, which is an alternate route back.) As you approach the road's end at what was once a parking area for autos and then a turnaround area for shuttle buses, you'll see that Mirror Lake is little more than a seasonal marsh. Tenaya Creek usually dries up by late September, and in former times the Park Service then would excavate up to thousands of tons of sand and gravel from the lake bed to be spread on snow-covered winter roads to make them more driveable. It was an efficient system, but declared environmentally incorrect and stopped in 1971. The lake, after all, was a short-lived rockfall-dammed lake made mirrorlike only with the addition of a dam and then kept deep enough for reflection with the annual removal of sediments.

Today visitors must console themselves with an unesthetic lake that usually does not mirror Tenaya Canyon, and upon drying, it exposes an unappealing, gravely floor. A grassy meadow may be a long time in coming, and if the manmade dam is removed, the creek

Mirror Lake as it appeared in 1976

will cut through the gravely floor, thereby lowering the water table, which would allow trees to invade the area and obscure all views.

To resume our loop hike, look for a trail that starts near the back end of the former parking area. (Since it is a heavily used, often smelly, horse trail, you might want to take the previously mentioned foot trail.) Starting south on the horse trail, we see, high above, North Dome and Half Dome. Next our trail passes myriad oversize bounders that fell from the vertical east wall of Washington Column. Soon our trail switchbacks briefly down to the paved road, then goes 100 yards west to a trail departing south toward nearby Tenaya Bridge. Our trail continues west another 100 yards to enter the unsigned Indian Caves area. Here you can find dozens of caves and dozens of house-size boulders. However, apparently there were too many climbing accidents and too much liability for the Park, so in the early '90s the area officially ceased to exist. If you bring children here, use the utmost caution. Before leaving this area, climb on top of a large, low slab that lies along the trail's north side to find Indian mortar holes used to pulverize acorns.

Continuing west you have a choice: either stay on the trail or take the paved bike path, just south of the caves. The two diverge and on this stretch you pass under the forbidding south face of Washington Column. Where the trail and bike path come together, near the northeast corner of the Group Camp, you can look up a deep cleft—weathered along a vertical fracture—which separates Washington Column from that giant lithic rainbow, Royal Arches.

After 150 yards of westward traverse our two parallel paths cross a very low "moraine." Actually, it is an old rockfall deposit similar to one immediately west of the Backpackers Walk-In Campground. About a two-minute walk past it we meet a southbound trail that divides the Group Camp on the east from the Backpackers Walk-In Campground on the west. Taking it you can save ⅓ mile, but by going west for a few minutes along the bike path (the trail goes to the Ahwahnee Hotel), we reach Sugarpine Bridge, named for a huge pine growing by its northeast corner. Like a royal arch, this stately giant could fall any day. From the southeast corner of the bridge we take a trail first southeast up the Merced River, then briefly northeast up Tenaya Creek. Where we meet the southbound trail we take it, immediately bridge Tenaya Creek, and walk southeast beside North Pines Campground to the Valley stables.

That first impression of the Valley—white water, azaleas, cool fir caverns, tall pines and stolid oaks, cliffs rising to undreamed-of heights, the poignant sounds and smells of the Sierra . . . was a culmination of experience so intense as to be almost painful.

—Ansel Adams

Day Hike 6
Valley Floor, Tenaya Canyon Loop

Distance: 5.1 mi (8.0 km) to 6.6 mi (10.6 km)

Grade: 2A, easy half-day hike

Trailhead: Same as for Day Hike 5. **D1.**

Introduction: In addition to visiting Mirror Lake, you get varying views of Half Dome and other features in deep, glacier-occupied Tenaya Canyon.

Description: If you hike to and return from Mirror Lake via the paved bike path—the most popular route—you will hike 5.1 miles. But if you follow all of Day Hike 5, you will hike 6.6 miles.

From just before the bike path's end at Mirror Lake you can descend a few steps to the lake's famous viewpoint. In former days, when the lake was deeper, early-morning visitors were treated to a reflection of Mt. Watkins in its still waters (See **Day Hike 5** for more on this dwindling lake.) Just north of these steps your Tenaya Canyon loop trail begins, and it quickly comes to the northwest arm of the seasonal lake. About 100 yards beyond it, where the trail bends right, you may see a cliff with polish imparted by a glacier before it retreated up-canyon about 14,500 years ago.

Up-canyon, our fairly level, forested trail soon approaches Tenaya Creek—a good picnic spot. Beyond it we go northeast toward the south spur of Mt. Watkins, which is occasionally seen. About 1.1 miles into our loop we come to a junction with a trail that switchbacks over 100 times in its 2,600-foot climb out of Tenaya Canyon and into its hanging tributary of Snow Creek, described in the *Hetch Hetchy* High Sierra Hiking Guide. Many believe that such canyons became hanging because trunk glaciers eroded their canyons far deeper than tributary glaciers did theirs. However, a hike up *treacherous* Tenaya Canyon would show that in its steepest parts, where glaciers flowed fastest and should have eroded most, the canyon retains its preglacial **V**-shaped cross section. So in your vicinity, where the floor is flat and glaciers flowed slower, erosion would have been less, and hence the **U**-shaped cross section is preglacial. And indeed, *unglaciated,* U-shaped Sierran canyons—trunk and hanging tributary—do exist.

At most you'll want to ascend only the first dozen switchbacks, an effort sufficient to get you above the canyon live oaks and present you with a view of Half Dome and much of Tenaya Canyon. From your vantage point in early summer, when the creek flows briskly, you ought to see Tenaya Creek falls, at about your elevation and about ½ mile up-canyon.

From the junction our loop trail again approaches the creek, and in ⅓ mile bridges it. Our return hike is along the east side of the creek, and it provides as pleasant a route as did our easy west-side route. About 1¼ miles from the creek's bridge we reach the east edge of Mirror Lake, then soon stroll past its dam, an artificial feature built around 1890 to add depth to the lake, which increased its photographic attributes. Just below the dam we descend to a pond that is gradually diminishing. In years past, it was one of the Valley's favorite swimming spots. Beyond it we leave the trail to Happy Isles and cross a footbridge to the bike path. Either descend it or take the longer route back, described in **Day Hike 5**.

Day Hike 7
Big Oak Flat Road Trail to Cascade Creek

Distance: 7.8 miles (12.6 km) round trip

Grade: 2C, strenuous half-day hike

Trailhead: From Crane Flat go east 6 miles toward Yosemite Valley down the new Big Oak Flat Road to the Foresta turnoff. Parking here is limited, so continue ¼ mile farther to the first turnout with a Yosemite Valley view. Park there and walk up to the Foresta road junction. This hike's distance is measured from the trailhead.

Introduction: During the late spring, when most of the Park's trails are under snow, this trail is at its best. Views are few and lakes are nonexistent, so it will appeal only to those who want an invigorating yet not exhausting walk and to those who especially focus on nature.

Description: The trail begins about 50 yards west of the Foresta road junction, and during spring harlequin lupines can abound here, identified by their pink-and-yellow flowers. Later on the flowers will be replaced by pea pods, and nearby Mariposa manzanitas, with their gray-green leaves, will have produced berries. The first third of our route was burned in a 1990 lightning-caused fire, which left charred snags, but it also allowed much more light to reach the ground—hence the profusion of shrubs and wildflowers. Particularly on an initial 400-foot, ½-mile climb to a ridge—which has views of El Capitan and Half Dome—dense herbs and shrubs can crowd the trail, and since this vegetation abounds in rodents, it is a prime habitat for rattlesnakes, so watch your step.

In the next ½ mile our trail briefly climbs the ridge, then traverses north to a moist area with a seasonal spring. Over the next ½ mile we enter unburned forest and then descend to usually flowing Wildcat Creek. Soon we begin to climb again, and do so for almost a mile until we start a short, steep descent along a ridge, which offers a view, across the Merced River canyon, of the Wawona Road traversing the flanks of Turtleback Dome. The steep descent continues down to nearby Tamarack Creek, which in summer flourishes with giant-leaved umbrella plants growing from its stream bed. At times this creek is a wet ford.

Again we make a mile-long climb, then make a momentary drop to a Cascade Creek tributary, which we boulder-hop only yards before reaching the old Big Oak Flat Road. At this creek crossing, service-berries hug the bank of a small pool fed by a photogenic cascade. Once on the road we have a brief walk down to the Cascade Creek bridge—a good spot for a lunch break (camping prohibited). In late summer the flow of Cascade Creek is slow and warm enough for safe and enjoyable splashing around in the small pools immediately downstream. During the summer, when the road to Tamarack Flat Campground is open, you'll want to take the much shorter **Day Hike 8** down to Cascade Creek.

The clearest way into the universe is through a forest wilderness
—John Muir

Day Hike 8
Tamarack Flat C.G. to Cascade Creek

Distance: 4.4 miles (7.1 km) round trip

Grade: 1B, easy half-day hike

Trailhead: From Crane Flat go northeast 3¾ miles up the Tioga Road to the Tamarack Flat Campground turnoff, immediately before the Gin Flat turnout. Go southeast 3¼ miles down the old Big Oak Flat Road to Tamarack Flat Campground's east end. Above **A1**.

Introduction: Around mid-morning Tamarack Flat Campground can become temporarily abandoned, only to receive another flood of motorized campers in the afternoon. Take the time to enjoy the campground during that tranquil part of day, and while you're in the vicinity, you might take the time to make this pleasant, easy hike.

Description: Some early visitors traveled by stagecoach to Yosemite Valley along this old road, completed it 1874. The first auto entered the Valley in 1900, and the route eventually became well-traveled until the completion of the new Big Oak Flat Road in 1940. Today, the road below the campground is closed to motor vehicles.

Tamarack Flat derives its name from its preponderance of "tamaracks," that is, lodgepole pines. However, as you leave the flat and hike across slopes on the old Big Oak Flat Road, white firs become dominant. Along both sides of the road are large, partly buried granitic boulders. These were not carried here by glaciers; instead, they developed in place, being resistant enough to subsurface weathering that they finally emerged on the surface quite intact, while the adjacent, less resistant, more fractured bedrock was chemically weathered and eroded away.

Just before you reach a prominent cluster of rocks your road begins a steady descent to Cascade Creek. At a switchback just 240 yards before the bridge across this creek, there is a junction with a trail, **Day Hike 7**, that comes from the new Big Oak Flat Road. Along the first 200 yards below its bridge, Cascade Creek splashes down low cascades into small pools, and in late summer these make nice "swimming holes." Before then the creek can be too swift for safe frolicking. Rooted in this creek are large-leaved umbrella plants, and growing just beside the water's edge are creek dog-woods, willows, western azaleas and service-berries.

Day Hike 9
El Capitan

Distance: 15.4 miles (24.8 km) round trip

Grade: 4D, strenuous day hike

Trailhead: Same as for Day Hike 8. Above **A1**.

Introduction: The vertical walls of 3,000-foot-high El Capitan attract rock climbers from all over the world, and more than five dozen extremely difficult routes ascend it. For nonclimbers this hike provides a much easier, safer way to attain El Capitan's summit, which stands only 15 feet above the north-side approach.

Description: Descend to Cascade Creek, as directed in **Day Hike 8**, then continue ½ mile down the old Big Oak Flat Road—now more like a trail—to a junction with Yosemite Valley's north rim trail. Here a major climb of almost 2,000 feet confronts us. Starting in a summer-warm forest, we climb hundreds of feet—steeply at times—up to drier slopes. We then encounter red firs, which grow near the top of a crest. Three miles from the trailhead, lodgepoles appear as we make a brief descent to a meadow, which we parallel to a crossing of a Ribbon Creek tributary. This we parallel east a mile down to Ribbon Creek. Ribbon Meadow, which we traverse on the first part of this descent, is more forest than meadow, and, where the route can become vague, blazes on lodgepoles guide you. Along the banks of Ribbon Creek are the trail's only acceptable campsites—but waterless when the creek dries up about midsummer. Now only 1¼ miles from our goal, we make a brief climb, an equally brief descent, and then an ascending traverse east to the top of El Capitan Gully.

Your first views of El Capitan and the south wall of Yosemite

El Capitan, the hard way: three climbers (arrows) about 1,000 feet up the monolith's prow

Valley appear on the traverse to the gully, and they continue as you climb south from it past dense shrubbery to a junction with the El Capitan spur trail. If you are hiking this trail after Ribbon Creek has dried up, you may want to continue on the main trail ½ mile northeast to two trickling springs. The trail beyond them is not all that interesting, but it does get you to Eagle Peak (the long way) and to Yosemite Creek (see **Day Hike 11**).

Along the spur trail south to El Capitan's broad, rounded summit, you can look up-canyon and identify unmistakable Half Dome, at the Valley's end, barely protruding Sentinel Dome, above the Valley's south wall, and fin-shaped Mt. Clark, on the skyline above the dome. Take your time exploring El Capitan's summit area, but don't stray too far. Even some top-notch climbers, after ascending a vertical route, have fallen to their deaths after unroping.

Day Hike 10
Yosemite Falls

Distance: 6.6 miles (10.6 km) round trip

Grade: 2D, strenuous half-day hike

Trailhead: Park in the westernmost part of the Yosemite Lodge parking lot close to the gas station, which is on the north side of the main road. **C1-D1.**

Introduction: Most Park visitors walk to the base of Lower Yosemite Fall. This popular trail (a knee-knocking descent in reverse) takes you to the other end—the brink of Upper Yosemite Fall. Like other early trails of Yosemite Valley, the Yosemite Falls trail was privately built and then was operated as a toll trail.

Description: From the gas station, pick any route along the east edge of Sunnyside Walk-In Campground and then continue upslope a minute or so to the north-side Valley floor trail (**Day Hike 2**). By walking west on it for a minute or so, you should reach the start of the Yosemite Falls trail. We leave conifers behind as we start up nearly four dozen switchbacks. Characteristic of old trails, each switchback leg is short. Under the shade of canyon live oaks, which dominate talus slopes like the one we're on, our so-far viewless ascent finally reaches a usually dry wash that provides us with framed views of Leidig Meadow and the Valley's central features.

With more than one fourth of the elevation gain below us, we pass by more oaks and an occasional bay tree as we now switchback east to a panoramic viewpoint, Columbia Rock, which is a worthy goal in itself. At its safety railing we can study the Valley's geometry, from Half Dome and the Quarter Domes west to the Cathedral Spires. Looking down on the Valley floor are some old, faint, abandoned meanders of the Merced River, carved before men stabilized its banks with large blocks. After a few gravely switchbacks climb from the viewpoint, the trail traverses northeast, drops slightly, then bends north for a sudden, dramatic view of Upper Yosemite Fall. West of the fall's lower section is a light scar 100 feet high, from which a 1,000-ton rock slab fell, after being struck by lightning in June 1976. In clear weather in November 1980, a 4,000-ton slab, probably weakened by the May 1980 Mammoth Lakes earthquakes, fell from a conspicuous scar on the cliffs west of and above the trail, killing three hikers. Smaller rockfalls have occurred, and over tens of millions of years countless rockfalls— not glacial erosion—widened the Valley.

Our climb up the long, steep trough ends among white firs and Jeffrey pines, about 135 switchbacks above the Valley floor. Here, in a gully beside a seasonal creeklet, our trail turns right while the Eagle Peak Trail, **Day Hike 11**, continues ahead. Our trail makes a brief climb east out of the gully and reaches a broad crest with several overused campsites. Their heavy use puts a strain on this area's vegetation, and it is best not to camp here. Along the crest we follow a trail south almost to the Valley's rim. Then at a juniper we veer east, descend steps almost to Yosemite Creek, and finally descend more steps to a fenced-in viewpoint. If you are acrophobic you should not attempt the last part of this descent, for it is possible, though unlikely, that you could slip on loose gravel and tumble over the brink. Beside the lip of Upper Yosemite Fall we see and hear it plunge all the way down its 1,430-foot drop to the rocks below. Just

Upper Yosemite Fall, from about switchback 89

Lost Arrow spire, first climbed in 1946

beyond the fall is a large roof, and beyond it stands the pride of the Clark Range, finlike Mt. Clark.

After returning to the crest campsites you can descend east to a bridge over Yosemite Creek and obtain water. However, be careful! Almost every year one or more persons, wading in it, slip on the glass-smooth creek bottom and are swiftly carried over the fall's brink. From the creek's bridge you could continue eastward ¾ mile up a trail to Yosemite Point. From that viewpoint a dramatic panorama extends from Clouds Rest south past Half Dome and Glacier Point, then west to the Cathedral Rocks. Near you a massive shaft of rock, Lost Arrow, rises almost to the Valley's rim, and beyond it you can see most of the switchbacking Yosemite Falls trail. See the *Hetch Hetchy* High Sierra Hiking Guide for trail description north from this viewpoint.

Day Hike 11
Eagle Peak

Distance: 12.4 miles (20.0 km) round trip

Grade: 3E, strenuous day hike

Trailhead: Same as for Day Hike 10. **C1-D1.**

Introduction: Strategically located Eagle Peak, highest of the Three Brothers, provides commanding views both up and down Yosemite Valley. The hike to it also provides exciting views, including some close-range ones of Upper Yosemite Fall.

Description: Follow **Day Hike 10** up to the Upper Yosemite Fall fenced-in viewpoint, then return to the trail junction in the gully west of the fall. From it we begin a shady trek north, climbing out of our gully, descending into a second, and climbing out of a third to a trail junction. Leaving the Yosemite Creek environs, we climb more than 300 feet, steeply at first, before leveling off in a bouldery area—part of a moraine. This moraine was deposited by a glacier that descended southwest from the west slopes of Mt. Hoffman. Now we turn south, generally leaving Jeffrey pines and white firs for lodgepole pines and red firs as we climb to Eagle Peak Meadows, whose north edge is blocked by an older moraine.

Beyond the sometimes boggy meadow we cross the headwaters of Eagle Peak Creek and in a few minutes reach a hillside junction. From it an old trail climbs and drops along a 1¾-mile course to the El Capitan spur trail. To reach the summit of that monolith, take the easier route starting from Tamarack Flat Campground (**Day Hike 9**). Branch left from the junction for a moderate ⅔-mile ascent to Eagle Peak's diminutive summit. From the weather-pitted, brushy summit 3,200 feet above the Valley floor, you get far-ranging views that extend all the way to the Sierra crest along the Park's east boundary. Below us, central Yosemite Valley spreads out like a map, and with this book's map you can identify many features.

Day Hike 12
Wawona Tunnel to Dewey Point

Distance: 10.9 miles (17.5 km) round trip

Grade: 3D, moderate day hike

Trailhead: Discovery View, at the east end of Wawona Tunnel, on the Wawona Road 1.5 miles west of the Bridalveil Fall parking lot entrance. **B1.**

Introduction: The trail takes you to five viewpoints: Inspiration, Old Inspiration, Stanford, Crocker, and Dewey. The first two, however, are somewhat blocked by vegetation. By hiking only to Stanford Point, you cut about 2½ miles and 900 feet of climbing from your hike. The creeks found along this route typically dry up by early summer, so make sure you bring sufficient water.

Description: Our signed trail starts at the west end of the south-side parking lot and makes a switchbacking, mostly viewless, 500-foot ascent for 0.6 mile to an intersection of the old Wawona Road. Built in 1875, this old stage route got a lot of use before it was closed with the opening of the newer Wawona Road in 1933. Today it provides a quiet descent 1.6 miles down to the newer road, meeting it just ⅓ mile above the entrance to the Bridalveil Fall parking lot.

Beyond the intersection, oaks and conifers shade us up another 500-foot ascent, but also hide most of the scenery. At Inspiration Point we meet a bend in the old Wawona Road, a point where early stage travelers got their first commanding view of El Capitan, Bridalveil Fall, and the Cathedral Rocks. Today incense-cedars, oaks, and pines obstruct the view. Pushing onward, we gain 1,200 feet on the Pohono Trail, encountering sugar pines, white firs, and sporadic Douglas-firs before arriving at Artist Creek. Now at an elevation with pleasant afternoon temperatures, we make a steep 300-foot climb to signed Old Inspiration Point, whose view is partly blocked. The actual point, identified on the map, is on the projecting spur below and northwest of us, and before construction of the old Wawona Road, a stock trail offered access to it.

Red firs now add shade to the forest canopy as we briefly ascend before dropping to a welcome spring and nearby Meadow Brook. If any water remains along this trail through midsummer, it will be found here. Beyond the creek and its alders we head north and soon descend to our first significant viewpoint, at the end of a short spur trail—Stanford Point. From it we see the gaping chasm of western Yosemite Valley and can easily identify its prominent landmarks: Leaning Tower, Bridalveil Fall, the Cathedral Rocks, El Capitan and, seasonally, Ribbon Fall. If you are not yet exhausted, the power of this view will urge you to climb ½ mile farther, reaching Crocker Point after more than 400 feet of elevation gain. This Point, on the brink of an overhanging cliff, provides a heart-pounding view similar to the last one, though better. Now most of the Valley's famed landmarks stand boldly before us, and we look over and beyond all the Cathedral Rocks to see the Three Brothers. To the left of Clouds Rest lie twin-towered Cathedral Peak and broad-topped Mt. Hoffmann, with distant Mt. Conness between them, marking the Sierra crest along the Park's northeast boundary.

For rival views, continue ⅔ mile to our hike's end at slightly higher Dewey Point. Now closer to the Cathedral Rocks, your perspective is different, and you look straight down the massive face that supports Leaning Tower. Also intriguing is the back side of

Middle Cathedral Rock, whose iron-rich, rust-stained surface stands out among the Valley's gray, somber colors. Finally, you see the Cathedral Spires head-on so they appear as one. Of these features, only Higher Cathedral Rock's summit, which arguably has the best views, can be reached (by ascending its south ridge) without needing a rope or fighting dense brush—*competent* hikers only.

Day Hike 13
Bridalveil Campground to Dewey Point

Distance: 10.0 miles (16.1 km) round trip

Grade: 3C, moderate half-day hike

Trailhead: Branch from the Wawona Road and drive 7.6 miles up the Glacier Point Road to the Bridalveil Creek Campground road. Turn right and drive 0.5 mile to the campground's entrance. **C2.**

Introduction: This is the easier of two routes to scenic Dewey Point, and it requires less than half the climbing effort of the previous hike. But then, it doesn't visit Stanford and Crocker points.

Description: At the entrance to Bridalveil Campground a closed road departs southwest away from the camp's Loop A. On it we soon cross a creek that drains Westfall Meadows, then immediately meet a trail. Heading south, this undesirable trail passes through these meadows, then makes a brush-choked descent to an old logging area—a 1920s "battleground" between environmentalists and the Yosemite Lumber Company. The environmentalists won, but the impact from logging lingers on.

Rather than head south we take a trail north, which climbs gently over old, weathered terrain to the Glacier Point Road. By starting here—¼ mile west of the campground's road—you would cut 1¾ miles off your round-trip distance. From the road the lodgepole-shaded trail gently descends almost to the north tip of largely hidden Peregoy Meadow before topping a low divide. Next it drops moderately and reaches a small cabin near the south edge of

McGurk Meadow. In this sedge-rich, sometimes flowery meadow (usually just after the snow has melted), our route bridges its creek.

From the meadow we see the low summits of the Ostrander Rocks to the east, and then at the meadow's north end re-enter dense lodgepole forest. Our trail soon crests at a shallow, viewless saddle, then descends moderately to gently to a low-crest trail fork. The fork right quickly joins the Pohono Trail and drops to Bridalveil Creek, with water year-round. We fork left, quickly join the Pohono Trail, start west on it and, near a broad, low divide (camping hereabouts), traverse a dry, gravely slope.

The forest cover now becomes dominated by firs, and on the damp shady floor beneath them you may find white-veined wintergreen, snow plant and spotted coralroot, all deriving nutrients to varying degrees from soil fungi. Two Bridalveil Creek tributaries are crossed, then a smaller third one before we start up a fourth that drains a curving gully. On its upper slopes Jeffrey pine, huckleberry oak, and greenleaf manzanita replace firs, and in a few minutes we reach prized Dewey Point, described at the end of **Day Hike 12**. If you can get someone to meet you at the Wawona Tunnel, then descend to it along this highly scenic portion of the Pohono Trail.

Day Hike 14
The Fissures at Taft Point

Distance: 2.6 miles (4.1 km) round trip

Grade: 1A, easy 2-hour hike

Trailhead: Branch from the Wawona Road and drive 13.2 miles up the Glacier Point Road to a scenic turnout, on your left, which is 2.3 miles before the Glacier Point parking-lot entrance. **D1.**

Introduction: The views from Taft Point rival those from Glacier Point. However, since Taft Point is reached by trail, it is much less visited than is Glacier Point. Generally lacking protective railings, Taft Point and the Fissures are potentially dangerous, so don't bring along children unless you can really keep them under strict control.

Description: From the road-cut parking area we descend about 50 yards to a trail, turn left, and start southwest on it. After about 150 yards of easy descent we pass a trailside outcrop that is almost entirely composed of glistening whitish-gray quartz. It also has small amounts of pink potassium feldspar. In a minute we come to seasonal Sentinel Creek, whose limited drainage area keeps Sentinel Fall downstream from being one of Yosemite Valley's prime attractions. After boulder-hopping the creek we follow an undulating trail west past pines, firs, and brush to a broad-saddle junction with the Pohono Trail (**Day Hike 16**). Just north of it you'll notice some large, weathered boulders. Not left by glaciers, these boulders weathered in place and will stand higher and higher above their surroundings as the bedrock is weathered away at a faster rate.

Sentinel Dome's lone Jeffrey pine, as it appeared in 1976

From the junction you descend to a sometimes seeping creeklet that drains through a small field of corn lilies. Descending toward the Fissures, you cross drier slopes that are generally covered with brush. Soon you arrive at the Fissures—five vertical, parallel fractures that cut through overhanging Profile Cliff, beneath your feet. Beyond them you walk up to a small railing at the brink of an obvious point and get an acrophobia-inducing view of overhanging Profile Cliff, beneath you. For the best views of Yosemite Valley and the High Sierra walk west to *exposed* Taft Point, from where you see the Cathedral spires and rocks, El Capitan, the Three Brothers, Yosemite Falls, and Sentinel Rock. Broad-topped Mt. Hoffmann stands on the skyline just east of Indian Canyon, and east of that peak stands distant Mt. Conness, on the Sierra crest.

Day Hike 15
Sentinel Dome

Distance: 2.4 miles (3.9 km) round trip

Grade: 1B, moderate 2-hour hike

Trailhead: Same as for the Hike 14 trailhead. **D1.**

Introduction: Sentinel Dome rivals Half Dome as the most-climbed dome in the Park. Tuolumne Meadows' Lembert and Pothole domes rival them, but neither is a true dome; each is a *roche moutonnée*—an asymmetrical, glacier-smoothed ridge. Indeed, most of the Sierra's domes, glaciated or unglaciated, are asymmetrical ridges.

Description: From the road-cut parking area we descend about 50 yards to a trail, turn right and make a curving, generally ascending traverse ¾ mile north almost to the south base of Sentinel Dome. Here we meet and briefly hike north on a road, then come to a fork, where we veer left, and in 30 yards, at another fork, veer left again. In a few minutes we arrive at the dome's north end, where we meet a path from Glacier Point. We now climb southwest up quite safe, unexposed bedrock slopes to the summit. Though a real trail to it doesn't exist, you should have no problems getting there.

At an elevation of 8,122 feet, Sentinel Dome is the second highest viewpoint above Yosemite Valley. Only Half Dome—a strenuous hike—is higher. Seen from the summit, El Capitan, Yosemite Falls, and Half Dome stand out as the three most prominent Valley landmarks. West of Half Dome are two bald features, North and Basket domes. On the skyline above North Dome stands blocky Mt. Hoffmann, the Park's geographic center, while to the east, above Mt. Starr King (an unglaciated, true dome) stands the rugged crest of the Clark Range. In years past almost everyone who climbed Sentinel Dome expected to photograph its windswept, solitary Jeffrey pine, made famous by Ansel Adams. That tree, unfortunately, finally succumbed to vandalism in 1984.

Day Hike 16
South Rim Traverse

Distance: 13.5 miles (21.7 km) one way

Grade: 3D, moderate day hike

Trailhead: Branch from the Wawona Road and drive 15.5 miles up the Glacier Point Road to its end. **D1.**

Introduction: This hike, the Pohono Trail, takes you past several excellent viewpoints, each showing a different part of Yosemite Valley in a unique perspective. After early June carry enough water (usually one quart) to last you until midpoint, Bridalveil Creek, which is the hike's only permanent source of water.

Description: On the low crest just east of the entrance to the Glacier Point parking lot, we start south up a signed trail that quickly forks. **Day Hike 18** branches left but we branch right and under white-fir cover momentarily cross the Glacier Point Road. Beyond it we immediately branch right again since the path ahead climbs to a ranger's residence. Our still-climbing trail curves west up to a switchback, then south to a road. This we cross and continue up the relentless grade to a north-descending crest which we cross before climbing briefly south to a gully. In it, almost a mile from Glacier Point, we are faced with a choice. Our route, the Pohono Trail, goes west to the brink of Sentinel Fall—usually dry by midsummer—while the alternate route, which starts north before climbing south, goes to scenic Sentinel Dome. Should you take the dome route, you can return to the Pohono Trail or you can take a more level route that adds ⅔ mile to your total distance. From the dome this route follows **Day Hike 15** in reverse, then the first half of **Day Hike 14**, which takes you back to the Pohono Trail.

Our main route, the Pohono Trail, leaves the gully, traverses southwest across a lower face of Sentinel Dome, then drops to a gravely gully with north-side boulders. The gravel and boulders are locally derived, not lingering deposits left by an ancient glacier, which nevertheless completely filled the Valley. Our route stays gravely on a short, sometimes steep descent to Sentinel Creek. There you can follow its bank 90 yards out to a point to get a good Valley view. Before mid-June hikers will see upper Sentinel Fall splashing down a chute immediately west of the point.

Beyond the seasonal creek we climb past lodgepole pines and white firs, and then, before a broad-saddle junction, past Jeffrey pines and red firs. At the junction we rejoin the alternate route and, as in the second half of **Day Hike 14**, descend a trail to the Fissures and Taft Point. Be careful when exploring this scenic though precipitous area. From the westernmost fissure the Pohono Trail descends south, then contours west to a low ridge. By following the ridge about 250 yards out to its end you'll reach an unnamed point that gives you a view down upon the Cathedral Rocks, lined up in a row. Descending from the low ridge, the shady Pohono Trail drops 700 feet to a bridge over Bridalveil Creek. Level ground is limited, so if you plan to camp, you can get water here, and perhaps camp in isolated spots on lands north and west of two nearby trail junctions.

From the creek, which is our hike's approximate midpoint, we climb shortly west to these two junctions with a lateral trail. This one climbs two miles south to the Glacier Point Road, then a short mile beyond it to Bridalveil Campground. This lateral trail constitutes the first half of **Hike 13** (described in the northward direction), and turning to the second half of that hike's description, we let it guide us over to Dewey Point. West from that point we follow **Hike 12**, described in the reverse direction, down to Discovery View, at the east end of Wawona Tunnel.

Day Hike 17
Glacier Point to Yosemite Valley via Four-Mile Trail

Distance: 4.5 miles (7.2 km) one way

Grade: 1A, easy 2-hour hike

Trailhead: Same as for Day Hike 16. **D1.**

Introduction: This trail provides a very scenic descent to Yosemite Valley—a descent that will acquaint you with the Valley's main features. This knee-knocking descent also gives you a feel for the Valley's 3,000-foot depth.

Description: Before building the Yosemite Falls trail (**Day Hike 10**) John Conway first worked on this trail, completing it in 1872. Originally about four miles long, it was rebuilt and lengthened in 1929 but the trail's name stuck. Our trail starts west from the north side of a concessionaire's shop, entering a shady bowl whose white firs and sugar pines usually harbor snow patches well into June. We then contour northwest, eventually emerge from forest shade and, looking east, see Glacier Point's two overhanging rocks capping a vertical wall. Soon we curve west, veer in and out of a cool gully, then reach a descending ridge. Switchbacks begin, and where gravel lies on hard tread, one can easily take a minor spill if not careful.

Brush dominates the first dozen switchback legs, thereby giving us unobstructed panoramas, though making the hike a hot one for anyone ascending from the Valley floor on a summer afternoon. However, as we duck east into a gully, shady conifers appear, though they somewhat censor our views. About midway down the series of switchbacks, canyon live oaks begin to compete with white firs and Douglas-firs, and our view is obstructed even more. After descending two thirds of the vertical distance to the Valley floor, our switchbacks temporarily end. A long, steady descent now ensues, mostly past canyon live oaks, whose curved-upward trunks are their response to creeping talus. Black oaks and incense-cedars also appear, and after ¼ mile we cross a creeklet that usually flows until early July. Down it we have an excellent view of Leidig Meadow.

Our steady descent again enters oak cover and we skirt below the base of imposing but largely hidden Sentinel Rock. At last a final group of switchbacks guide us down to a former parking loop, closed about 1975, and we proceed north, intersecting the Valley floor's southside trail, **Day Hike 2**, halfway to our end point, the eastbound road.

Day Hike 18

Glacier Point to Yosemite Valley via Nevada and Vernal Falls

Distance: 9.1 miles (14.6 km) one way

Grade: 2C, moderate day hike

Trailhead: Same as for Day Hike 16. **D1.**

Introduction: This is the most scenic of all trails descending to the floor of Yosemite Valley. Either take a bus up to Glacier Point or have someone drop you there and meet you down at Camp Curry.

Description: Just east of the entrance to the Glacier Point parking lot, we start south up a signed trail that quickly forks. The Pohono Trail, **Day Hike 16**, veers right, but we veer left, climbing a bit more before starting a moderate descent. A switchback leg helps ease the grade, and then we descend, often with views. A 1987 natural fire blackened most of the forest from near the trailhead to just beyond the upcoming Buena Vista Trail junction, but most trees survived. In open areas, black oaks are thriving, and shrubs have regenerated with a vengeance. Between charred trunks are occasional great views of Half Dome, Mt. Broderick, Liberty Cap, Nevada Fall, and Mt. Starr King. After 1⅔ miles and an 800-foot drop, our Glacier

Point-Panorama Trail meets the Buena Vista Trail. Over 2.2 miles this first heads up-canyon to Illilouette Creek, then leads up along it to intersect the Mono Meadow Trail (**Backpack Hike 4**).

Our trail branches left and switchbacks down to a spur trail that goes a few yards to a railing. Here, atop an overhanging cliff, we get an unobstructed view of 370-foot-high Illilouette Fall, which splashes down over a low point on the rim of massive Panorama Cliff. Behind it Half Dome rises boldly while above Illilouette Creek Mt. Starr King rises even higher. In ¼ mile our trail descends to a wide bridge, wisely placed upstream. Still, wading in the creek could carry you swiftly downstream and over the fall.

Our trail soon passes just above the brink of Illilouette Fall, and gravels here are remnants of a thick accumulation that choked the creek when the uppermost part of the last glacier formed a low ice-dam across its mouth. The trail then starts a major climb along the slopes just above Panorama Cliff. It first climbs briefly along its rim, then switchbacks away, soon returning near Panorama Point. The former viewpoint was in part undermined by a monstrous rockfall that broke loose during the winter of 1968–69. The rest of the viewpoint could break loose at any time. About ⅓ mile past this vicinity we have a superlative panorama extending from Upper Yosemite Fall east past Royal Arches, Washington Column, and North Dome to Half Dome. Our forested, moderate climb ends after 200 more feet of elevation gain, and then we descend gently to the rim for some more views, contour east and have even more, these dominated by Half Dome, Mt. Broderick, Liberty Cap, Clouds Rest, and Nevada Fall. Our contour ends at a junction with the Mono Meadow Trail, which climbs southwest over a low ridge before descending to Illilouette Creek.

Beyond the junction we make a mile-long, switchbacking, generally viewless descent to a trail split, each branch descending a few yards to the John Muir Trail. You'll descend along it, as described in the last part of **Day Hike 20**, but first walk over to the nearby brink of roaring Nevada Fall.

Alternately, you could descend the Mist Trail, a shorter route, which begins a few hundred yards northeast of Nevada Fall. Being shorter, it is also steeper, and is potentially dangerous for those who try to descend it too rapidly. This wet route is described in the opposite direction in the first part of **Day Hike 20**. From the reunion of the John Muir and the Mist trails, you walk but a minute to the Vernal Fall bridge, then follow **Day Hike 19** in reverse down to the Happy Isles shuttle-bus stop. From it you can ride or walk west to Camp Curry, the Valley's east hub of activity.

Day Hike 19
Vernal Fall Bridge

Distance: 1.6 miles (2.6 km) round trip

Grade: 1A, moderate 2-hour hike

Trailhead: Happy Isles shuttle-bus stop in eastern Yosemite Valley. **D1.**

Introduction: Paved paths to near the bases of Yosemite and Bridalveil falls, and one to this bridge, are all very popular. If you have only one day here, take all three. The paved trail to the bridge, however, is steep—intimidating for out-of-shape flatlanders.

Description: From the shuttle-bus stop you head south across a shady flat to the Happy Isles area, which has the informative Happy Isles Trail Center. Nearby you cross a bridge, and at its east end reach a stream-gaging station. From this station the famous John Muir Trail heads about 210 miles southward to the summit of Mt. Whitney. After a few minutes up it we meet a trail on our right that descends to upper Happy Isle. In a few more yards we reach a small spring with questionably pure water.

Beyond it the climb south steepens, and before bending east we get a glance back at Upper Yosemite Fall, partly blocked by the Glacier Point Apron. This smooth, curving apron contrasts with the generally angular nature of Yosemite's topography. Note the canyon wall south of the apron, which has a series of oblique-angle cliffs—all of them remarkably similar in orientation since they've fractured along the same series of joint planes. At the canyon's end Illilouette Fall plunges 370 feet over a vertical, joint-controlled cliff. Just east of the fall is a large, light-colored scar that marks the site of a major rockfall that broke loose during the winter of 1968–69.

Climbing east we head up a canyon whose floor in times past was buried by as much as 3,500 feet of glacier ice. Hiking beneath the unstable, highly fractured south wall of Sierra Point, we cross a talus slope—an accumulation of rockfall boulders. The May 1980 Mammoth Lakes earthquakes perhaps set up three rockfalls here, which finally occurred in conjunction with heavy rains in late spring 1986. More may occur. Entering forest shade once more, we first struggle up the steep trail before making a quick drop to our destination, the Vernal Fall bridge. From it we see Vernal Fall—a broad curtain of water—plunge 320 feet over a vertical cliff before cascading toward us. Looming above the fall are two glacier-resistant masses, Mt. Broderick (left) and Liberty Cap (right). Just beyond our bridges are restrooms and an emergency telephone (heart attacks, slips on dangerous rocks). **Day Hike 20** continues onward.

Day Hike 20
Vernal-Nevada Falls Loop

Distance: 5.9 miles (9.5 km) semiloop trip

Grade: 2D, strenuous half-day hike

Trailhead: Same as for Day Hike 19. **D1.**

Introduction: Mile for mile, this very popular hike may be the most scenic one in the Park. The first part of this loop goes up the famous (or infamous) Mist Trail—a steep, strenuous trail that sprays you with Vernal Fall's mist, which cools you on hot afternoons but makes the mostly bedrock route slippery and dangerous. Take rain gear or, if it is a warm day, strip down to swimwear, since you can dry out on slabs above the fall. For best photos start after 10 a.m.

Description: Day Hike 19 tells you what to expect along your hike up to the Vernal Fall bridge. About 200 yards beyond the bridge we come to the start of our loop. Here the Mist Trail continues upriver while the John Muir Trail starts a switchbacking ascent to the right.

This is the route taken by those with horses or other pack stock. We'll go up the Mist Trail and down the John Muir Trail. You can, of course go up or down either, but by starting the loop up the Mist Trail, you stand less chance of an accident. Hikers are more apt to slip or to twist an ankle descending than ascending, and the Mist Trail route to Nevada Fall has ample opportunities for mishaps.

In swimsuit or raingear we start up the Mist Trail and soon, rounding a bend, receive our first spray. If you're climbing this trail on a sunny day, you're almost certain to see one, if not two, rainbows come alive in the fall's spray. The spray increases as we advance toward the fall, but we get a brief respite behind a large boulder. Beyond it we complete our 300-plus steps, most of them wet, which guide us up through a verdant, spray-drenched garden. We struggle up the last few dozen steps under the shelter of trees, then, reaching an alcove beneath an ominous overhang, scurry left up a last set of stairs. These, protected by a railing, guide us to the top of a vertical cliff. Pausing here we can study our route, the nearby fall, and the river gorge. Our railing ends near the brink of Vernal Fall, but unfortunately, people venture beyond it, and every year it seems that one or more are swept over the fall.

Plunging into the upper end of chilly Emerald Pool is churning Silver Apron. Late in the summer when the Merced's flow is noticeably down, one is tempted to glide down this watery chute into Emerald Pool. This is hazardous, for one can easily crash on some boulders just beyond the end of this silvery chute. Rivers are not to be taken lightly. You'll see a bridge spanning the narrow gorge that confines the Silver Apron, and this structure is our immediate goal. The trail can be vague in this area for so many paths have been trampled through it, but our route leaves the river near the pool's far (east) end, and you'll find outhouses here. After a brief climb south, the trail angles east to a nearby junction. From it a view-packed trail climbs almost ½ mile to Clark Point, where it meets the John Muir Trail. We, however, stay low and curve left over to the Silver Apron bridge. Beyond it we have a short, moderate climb up to a broad bench which was once the site of La Casa Nevada. Opened in 1870 it was managed by Albert Snow until 1891, when a fire burned the main structure to the ground.

Spurred onward by the sight and sound of plummeting Nevada Fall, we climb eastward, soon commencing a series of more than two dozen compact switchbacks. As we ascend them, Nevada Fall slips out of view, but we can see towering Liberty Cap. Our climb ends at the top of a joint-controlled gully where, on brushy slopes, we once again meet the John Muir Trail (with outhouses just up it). From this junction we head southwest toward nearby Nevada Fall. Along this stretch you may notice boulders—rich in large, blocky feldspar crystals—that contrast strongly with the local bedrock. These boulders are *erratics*—that is, rocks left by retreating glaciers which were here perhaps as recently as 13,500 years ago. Nearing the Merced River you may also notice patches of bedrock that have been polished, striated, and gouged by the last glacier.

Just a few yards before the Nevada Fall bridge you can strike northwest on a short, easily missed spur trail down to a viewpoint beside the fall's brink. This viewpoint's railing is seen from the fall's bridge, thereby giving you an idea where the trail ends. Don't go straying along the cliff's edge and, as mentioned earlier, respect the river—people have been swept over this fall too. Standing near the tumultuous brink of the Merced River, you can look across its canyon—minimally eroded by glaciers—to Glacier Point. Vernal Fall, which lies just beyond Emerald Pool, plunges over a vertical wall that is perpendicular to the steep one Nevada Fall plunges over. This part of the canyon contains major fracture planes, or joint planes, which account for the canyon's angular landscape.

From the Nevada Fall bridge we strike southwest, immediately passing more glacier polish and erratic boulders, and shortly ending a gentle ascent at a junction just beyond a seeping spring. Here we meet the Glacier Point-Panorama Trail, and those descending from Glacier Point (**Day Hike 18**) join us here for a descent to Happy Isles along the John Muir Trail. We start with a high traverse that provides an ever-changing panorama of domelike Liberty Cap and broad-topped Mt. Broderick—both testaments to the ineffectiveness of glacial erosion. As we progress west, Half Dome becomes prominent, its hulking mass vying for our attention. Eventually we descend to Clark Point, where we meet a scenic connecting trail that switchbacks down to Emerald Pool.

Liberty Cap and 594-foot-high Nevada Fall

Backpackers, packers, and those wishing to keep dry continue down the John Muir Trail, which curves south into a gully, switchbacks down to the base of spreading Panorama Cliff, then switchbacks down a talus slope. Largely shaded by canyon live oaks and Douglas-firs, it reaches a junction with a horse trail (no hikers allowed) that descends to the Valley's stables. We continue a brief minute more to a junction with the Mist Trail, turn left and quickly reach the Vernal Fall bridge, from which we retrace our steps.

Day Hike 21
Half Dome via Little Yosemite Valley

Distance: 16.4 miles (26.4 km) round trip

Grade: 4E, strenuous day hike

Trailhead: Same as for Day Hike 19. **D1.**

Introduction: Half Dome "is a crest of granite rising to the height of 4,737 feet above the Valley, perfectly inaccessible, being probably the only one of all the prominent points about the Yosemite which never has been and never will be trodden by human foot." So wrote Josiah D. Whitney—California's first prominent geologist—in *The Yosemite Guide-Book* (1870). Just five years later the impossible was accomplished, when George Anderson labored for weeks drilling a row of holes up to the "inaccessible" summit, reached on October 12, 1875. In the 1990s, *hundreds* reach the summit virtually every sunny summer *day*. The dome is being loved to death, and perhaps the day will come when the cables up it will be dismantled, leaving the summit to the realm of climbers.

Description: Try to start by 7 a.m., following **Day Hike 20** up the Mist Trail or the John Muir Trail to a junction just northeast of the brink of Nevada Fall. If you take the former, you will save 1.0 mile. From the junction and its adjacent outhouses we ascend a brushy, rocky gully, then quickly descend, reaching both forest shade and the Merced River. Beneath pines, firs, and incense-cedars we continue northeast along the river's azalea-lined bank, then quickly reach a trail fork. The left fork saves you 0.1 mile, but you'll expend as much energy as on the right fork due to the climb to vault Liberty Cap's low east ridge. We keep to the main trail and go a short ½ mile to another junction, from where the John Muir Trail/Half Dome Trail branches north, while the Merced Lake Trail continues east. On the short stretch north to the left fork, you pass first a large camping area with bearproof storage boxes, then outhouses, and beyond them a spur trail northeast over to a rangers' camp. Some hikers on their way to Half Dome or Merced Lake (**Backpack Hike 1**) spend their first night here.

From the junction with the left fork, you've not yet expended half the energy required to reach the summit. After 1⅓ miles of forested ascent you leave the John Muir Trail, which climbs east to Tuolumne Meadows (see the *Tuolumne Meadows* High Sierra Hiking Guide), and continue up the Half Dome Trail. After 0.6 mile you meet a spur trail that goes about 280 yards east to a spring— your last chance for water (treat it!). The trail bends west before reaching a saddle, and then it climbs through a forest of red firs and Jeffrey pines instead of white firs and incense-cedars. Half Dome's northeast face comes into view and, topping a crest, we get a fine view of Clouds Rest and its satellites, the Quarter Domes. Between them and us, previous glaciers spilled into Tenaya Canyon.

A crest traverse reveals more views, then it ends all too soon at the base of Half Dome's shoulder, where a sign warns us of the potential lightning hazard. Even when thunderstorms are miles away, static electricity can build up on the summit. Out of a clear blue sky a charge can bolt down the cable, throwing your arms off it—or worse. If your hair starts standing on end, beat a hasty retreat!

Almost two dozen short switchbacks guide us up the view-blessed ridge of the dome's shoulder and, near the top, a cable lends additional aid. A real danger on this section is loose gravel, which could prove fatal if you fell off the trail at an exposed spot. Topping the shoulder we are confronted with the famous, intimidating Half Dome cables. (Usually the cables are put up around mid-May and removed in early October.) The ascent starts out gently enough, but it too quickly steepens almost to a 45° angle. On this stretch,

Hikers descending Half Dome's intimidating cable route

first-timers often slow to a snail's pace, clenching both cables with sweaty hands.

The rarefied air certainly hinders our progress as we struggle upward, but an easing gradient gives new incentive and soon we are scrambling up to the broad summit area about the size of 17 football fields. With caution most hikers proceed to the dome's high point (8,842 feet), located at the north end, from where they can view the dome's overhanging northwest point. Stout-hearted souls peer over the lip of this point for an adrenaline-charged view down the dome's 2,000-foot-high northwest face, perhaps seeing climbers ascending it. In the past a few folks liked to camp overnight to view the sunrise, but in 1993 camping became banned in order to protect the small population of Mt. Lyell salamanders.

From the broad summit of this monolith, which originated in the late days of the dinosaurs, you have a 360° panorama. You can look down Yosemite Valley to the bald brow of El Capitan and up Tenaya Canyon past Clouds Rest to Cathedral Peak, the Sierra crest, and Mt. Hoffmann. Mt. Starr King—a dome that rises only 250 feet above us—dominates the Illilouette Creek basin to the south, while the Clark Range cuts the sky to the southeast. Looking due east across Moraine Dome's summit, one sees Mt. Florence, whose broad form hides the Park's highest peak, Mt. Lyell, behind it.

Day Hike 22
Alder Creek Trail to Bishop Creek

Distance: 6.3 miles (10.2 km) round trip

Grade: 2C, moderate half-day hike

Trailhead: On the Wawona Road 3.9 miles north of the Wawona Campground entrance and 280 yards west of the Alder Creek crossing; also 7.4 miles south of the Glacier Point Road junction. **B4.**

Introduction: Your descent to Bishop Creek can be one of the Sierra's most pleasant springtime hikes, though by early summer the creeks run dry and temperatures soar. Most of this trail's length is across rolling topography carpeted with one of the author's favorite plants, mountain misery; nowhere else in the Park will you see such a spread of this low, aromatic shrub.

Description: From the road's bend near a cut through weathered granite, our trail drops below the Wawona Road and parallels it northwest. The trail quickly widens along an abandoned road, which it soon leaves. After about ½ mile of traversing, it begins a long drop to the South Fork Merced River. About 1.2 miles from our trailhead, we leave the Park and in the Sierra National Forest descend 0.8 mile to a springtime creek. In a short ¼ mile beyond it we climb to a low ridge, on which you'll find about a half dozen Indian mortar holes, perhaps covered with black-oak leaves, just a few yards west of the trail. From the ridge we have a steady descent, one that winds in and out of gullies as it drops about 550 feet to the banks of Bishop Creek. From there you could continue down to the South Fork Merced River—a total drop of almost 800 feet along a dry, steep 1.4-mile course. However, the steepness, heat, riverside litter, and springtime ticks make the descent not worth it.

Day Hike 23
Chilnualna Falls

Distance: 8.1 miles (13.0 km) round trip

Grade: 2D, moderate day hike

Trailhead: At the east end of the Chilnualna Road. The Chilnualna Road starts in the Wawona area immediately north of the bridge across the South Fork Merced River. On it you drive past the Pioneer Yosemite History Center and a nearby fork right to the Park's district office. In 0.1 mile another road forks left, and just beyond it, on the right, is a small parking area for the Alder Creek Trail, located ½ mile along your road. This northbound trail begins roughly 100 yards east of the road forking left. You then drive east 1¼ miles farther, to a short road branching down to a large parking area. This road is located only 100 yards before the pavement on Chilnualna Road ends. Ahead, a dirt road descends to bridge Chilnualna Creek, while a paved road curves northwest. From the parking area a trail climbs about 100 yards north-northeast to the actual trailhead. If you have stock, you will have to head about 250 yards up the paved road curving northwest to a road climbing north. Ascend this ¼ mile to its second switchback, from where a horse trail climbs about 280 yards east to the end of the foot trail. **C5.**

Introduction: Not all waterfalls are found in Yosemite Valley; several are located along Chilnualna Creek. As in the Valley, the severely hanging canyon of Chilnualna Creek above the highest fall originated tens of millions of years ago, *not* in response to glaciers deeply eroding the South Fork Merced River canyon, because they didn't do that.

Description: The hikers' trail starts as a gently ascending dirt road, quickly giving way to a footpath that heads up Chilnualna Creek almost to its 25-foot-high fall. When the creek's flow is *slow*, hikers *with some climbing skill* can follow the creek several hundred yards up to a fairly large swimming hole, at the base of another fall. Most stick to the trail, which becomes steep and potentially dangerous, especially when wet. Soon it reaches the horse trail, and on it we climb to cross a manzanita-clothed ridge before entering a forest of ponderosa pines and incense-cedars. A few open spots allow us to survey the Wawona area to the south, Wawona Point to the southeast, and Wawona Dome to the east. Then climbing east we reach Chilnualna Creek in ¼ mile, and hike up along it another ¼ mile. If you need water, get it before the trail leaves the creek. In mid and late summer the ascent can be hot and dry.

On a moderately graded trail we now climb more than a dozen switchbacks of various lengths up into a cooler forest before making a fairly open traverse southeast toward the main Chilnualna Fall. Here we see the entire length of the fall, which churns for hundreds of feet down a deep, confining chute. Our trail comes to within a few yards of the fall's brink, but due to loose gravel and lack of a protective railing, you should not venture any closer to it.

Not far above Chilnualna Fall proper is an upper fall, a 60-foot-high cascade that is quite impressive in early season. To get around this fall and its small gorge, our trail switchbacks north, then curves south above the lip of the gorge. Views extending over the forested Wawona area are left behind as we reach a trail junction. Just below this junction and also below the main trail east of it are several good campsites. From the junction **Backpack Hike 5** follows the trail climbing generally northeast up Chilnualna Creek, while **Backpack Hike 2** follows the trail that descends south to here from Turner Meadows.

Day Hike 24
Wawona to Mariposa Grove

Distance: 16.2+ miles (26.0+ km) round trip

Grade: 4D, strenuous day hike

Trailhead: In Wawona, take the eastbound road that goes along the south side of the South Fork Merced River. This first passes a parking area on the right, then soon reaches an RV dump station on the left. Continue east 160 yards farther to a road branching right, west-southwest. Make a tight turn onto it and follow it to where it curves south and almost levels off. The trail begins immediately before the road crosses the high point of a west-dropping ridge. **B5.**

Introduction: Though almost all Mariposa Grove visitors drive to it, one can also walk to it. This hike describes the forested pathway to the Mariposa Grove of Big Trees (giant sequoias)—or Wawona, as the Indians called them.

Description: Our trail, initially part of the Two Hour Ride Trail, begins eastward as a dusty horse trail locally adorned with excrement, urine, and flies. We quickly pass an old, abandoned canal, climb to the crest, and in a short mile reach a crest fork. To the left, a broad horse path descends to a summer camp. From it the broad horse path climbs southeast back up to a junction with our trail. This junction is reached after a second short, dusty mile, most of it right along the forested crest. Views of large Wawona meadow are generally poor or nonexistent. From the saddle where the broad horse path rejoins our trail, we turn south to briefly descend to within 40 yards of noisy, paved Wawona Road, where there is parking for several vehicles. Starting from here cuts 1.9 miles, each way, from the total distance.

Here the Two Hour Ride Trail leaves us, crossing Wawona Road to loop back to the Wawona area. Now on a much less used, generally horse-free route, we climb east up a steepening ridge before veering south up to a usually flowing creek, 1.7 miles beyond the horse trail. Our trail maintains its moderate gradient as it next climbs south above the headwalls of two eroding, enlarging bowls. Then in ½ mile it begins to switchback up to a broad-crest junction with a ridge trail, about 6¼ miles from your trailhead.

The most direct way from here to the heart of the sequoia grove—its museum—is the following 1.3-mile route. Head 0.8 mile northeast up the Outer Loop Trail to a junction in a fairly level area, branch right and go about 150 yards southeast to cross the grove's tram road, continue 0.2 mile east on another trail, then branch left onto another trail that winds about 250 yards eastward to the museum.

The preferred way is longer, making a 3.7-mile loop. Start south on the Outer Loop Trail, which soon begins a winding, rolling traverse ½ mile southwest over to a junction with a northeast-climbing trail, then leads 0.1 mile farther to another junction. Branch left, leaving the Outer Loop Trail, to traverse ½ mile to the tunneled California Tree, then in 50 yards reach the famed Grizzly Giant. From it a trail climbs 250 yards north to a crossing of the tram road. This road makes an initial climb southwest to a switchback, from which a minor trail drops southeast, then climbs briefly to a trail paralleling the tram road northwest. You keep to the main trail and make a winding, 400-foot ascent for ¾ mile to the tram road. From here you'll see the museum, and hiking toward it, you first start north on a trail that quickly reaches a junction, from which you wind about 250 yards eastward to the museum. Complete the loop hike by following the previous paragraph in reverse. There are other trails, some worth taking, some not, but all adding to your distance. These are mentioned in **Day Hike 25.**

Day Hike 25
Mariposa Grove of Big Trees

Distance: 6.9 miles (11.0 km) loop trip; other routes possible

Grade: 2C, moderate half-day hike

Trailhead: From the Park's south entrance station drive east 2.1 miles up to road's end at the Big Trees parking lot. Be forewarned that by mid-morning it can be full. During summer and early fall, take the free shuttle bus that leaves from the Wawona Store, just northwest of the Wawona Hotel. **C5.**

Introduction: Near the southwest end of the parking lot is an information kiosk in which visitors can get introduced to the Mariposa Grove while waiting to take the tram. The tram ride gives you an instructive, guided tour of the grove's salient features and, at its stops, you can get off, explore the immediate area, and then get on the next tram. However, by hiking you get a more intimate experience with the giant sequoia and associated plants and animals.

Description: Two trails leave from the eastern, upper end of the parking lot. The northern one is the Outer Loop Trail, which makes a switchbacking climb 0.6 mile north to a junction with a trail east, then a winding climb 0.6 mile northwest to a junction with a trail down to Wawona (see **Day Hike 24**). Our route is the southern one, which actually starts at the kiosk and runs along the edge of the parking lot. On this nature trail we momentarily parallel the tram road east before crossing a creeklet and the road. The signs along this trail not only identify the notable sequoias, but also educate you on their natural history, including such items as bark, cones, fire, reproduction, and associated plants and animals.

One point worth elaborating is how difficult it is for a sequoia to successfully replace itself. For a seed to become a tree first there must be a fire, which removes humus to expose mineral soil. Then for the seedling to survive, there must be adequate soil moisture. In the last 2½ million years—the Ice Age—summers have been too dry, and almost invariably seedlings die before fall rains arrive. Before then, summers were wetter, especially before 15 million

A giant-sequoia cone, ⅔ life size

years ago. Today, a seedling is likely to survive only if first there has been a ground fire and then if there has been a heavy snowpack so that the soil will stay moist through the summer. Fortunately, a sequoia can live to 2,000+ years in age, producing over a *half billion* seeds in this time, and only one seed is required to replace the parent. The oldest known sequoia—the Muir snag, in the Kings River's Converse Basin Grove—is estimated to have lived for about 3,500 years. Sequoias survive because they have "all the time in the world" to wait for proper regenerative conditions.

At the tram-road crossing lies the Fallen Monarch, largely intact, including its roots. Note that they grew in shallow soil, because bedrock lies only a couple of feet down. Unfortunately, occasional severe winds can topple a tree before it reaches old age. From the south side of the road our nature trail climbs ¼ mile east before crossing the road. At this spot stand the Bachelor and the Three Graces. In a similar distance our trail reaches the Grizzly Giant. Like the Leaning Tower of Pisa, this still-growing giant seems ready to fall any second, and one wonders how such a top-heavy, shallow-rooted specimen could have survived as long as it has. Though the largest tree in the Park—and probably the oldest at almost 3,000 years—there are at least 25 specimens elsewhere larger than it. It has a trunk volume of about 34,000 cubic feet, compared to about 52,500 cubic feet for the largest, the General Sherman, in Sequoia National Park's Giant Forest Grove. The Grizzly Giant has enough timber to build about 20 homes, but fortunately sequoia wood is very brittle, shattering when a tree falls—a feature that saved it from being logged into oblivion.

Heading north from the east end of the enclosure circling the Grizzly Giant, we reach in 50 yards the California Tree, also enclosed, but with a path through it. It once had a deep burn, which was cut away in 1895 so that tourists could ride a stage through it. Beyond this tree a trail traverses ½ mile west to the Outer Loop Trail. We, however, take an ascending trail that parallels the tram road north for 250 yards before crossing it. Our trail then climbs to a nearby switchback from where a lightly used trail winds southeast down to an old road. We start north and quickly reach a lackluster trail that traverses northwest to the tram road, from where another trail, equally lackluster, descends southwest to the Outer Loop Trail. Additionally a switchbacking one climbs northeastward to a loop in the upper part of the tram road.

> Walk the Sequoia woods at any time of the year and you will say they are the most beautiful and majestic on earth. Beautiful and impressive contrasts meet you everywhere—the colors of tree and flower, rock and sky, light and shade, strength and frailty, endurance and evanescence. . . .
>
> —John Muir

Our trail gains 400 feet elevation climbing to the same spot, starting north and then going briefly east before switchbacking to wind northwest to the upper end of the switchbacking trail, the junction being about 15 yards from the tram road. Here too is the Upper Loop Trail, which parallels the tram road counterclockwise as both circle the upper grove. (Although our area is called the Mariposa Grove, it is really two groves, a lower one from the Grizzly Giant and below, and an upper one encircled by the Upper Loop Trail.)

This guide's suggested route from the junction is to start on a trail a few paces away, which descends north about 90 yards to a junction with an east-west trail (along the most direct way to the Mariposa Grove Museum in **Day Hike 24**). This winds about 250 yards eastward, skirting below restrooms and then passing a west-heading nature trail before reaching the museum, with an adjacent water fountain. In the museum you will find information and displays on the giant sequoia, its related plants and animals, and the area's history. From just east of it you could take a trail ⅓ mile east up to the tram road, beside which you'd spy the lower end of the Fallen Wawona (Tunnel) Tree, which fell during the late winter or spring of 1969. This 2,200-year-old giant, like many others, had a fire-scarred base, and it was enlarged in 1881 for first stagecoaches and much later automobiles to pass through it. An old timer is one who remembers waiting in a long line while each car drove through, stopping to have a passenger get out and photograph the momentous event. Today, the tree is not much to look at.

The suggested route continues from the museum momentarily east along the tram road to a bend. Here is the amazing Telescope Tree, which has been hollowed out by fire. Inside it you can look straight up to the heavens. Despite its great internal loss, this tree is still very much alive, for its vital fluids—as in all trees—are conducted in the sapwood, immediately beneath the thick bark. The heartwood is just dead sapwood whose function is support.

From the back side of the tree you take a trail that climbs 50 yards to the Upper Loop Trail, mentioned earlier. On it you hike ⅓ mile counterclockwise to pass just above the Fallen Wawona Tree,

The museum is dwarfed by giant sequoias

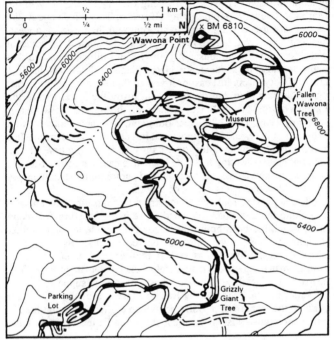

Topographic map of the Mariposa Grove, scale 1:24,000

then continue about 250 yards to a crest saddle. Just 40 yards east of it is the Galen Clark Tree, a fine specimen named for the man who first publicized this grove and later became its first guardian. From the saddle a road branches from the tram-road loop, and on it we make an easy climb ½ mile to Wawona Point. No sequoias grow along this route, probably because of insufficient ground water. From the point we see the large, partly man-made meadow at Wawona, to the northwest, and the long, curving cliff of Wawona Dome, breaking a sea of green, to the north.

After returning to the crest saddle, we descend west along the Outer Loop Trail, which takes us down almost 3 essentially viewless, sequoia-less miles to the parking lot. The descending trail winds westward about 0.7 mile to a junction. From here a connecting trail goes about 270 yards southeast down to the tram road and the adjacent west end of the nature trail. Onward the Outer Loop Trail descends about 200 yards to a second connecting trail, the one mentioned in **Day Hike 24**, descending about 150 yards southeast to cross the grove's tram road. We continue 0.8 mile southwest on the Outer Loop Trail down to the junction on a broad ridge from where one could follow **Day Hike 24** in reverse 6¼ miles down to Wawona. Instead, we start south on the Outer Loop Trail, which soon begins a winding, rolling traverse ½ mile southwest over to a junction with a northeast-climbing trail, then walk 0.1 mile farther to another junction, the eastbound trail from it leading to the California Tree and the Grizzly Giant. Unless you want to make another visit to them (and add about ½ mile to your hike) continue southward ½ mile down to the parking lot.

Backpack Hike 1
Merced Lake via Little Yosemite Valley

Distance: 28.2 miles (45.4 km) round trip

Grade: 5E, moderate 3-day hike

Trailhead: Just east of the day-use parking lot in Curry Village, drive 0.2 mile southeast along the shuttle-bus road to a short spur road branching right to a backpackers' parking lot. **D1.**

Introduction: Best done in three days with overnight stops at Little Yosemite Valley and Merced Lake, this hike is often done in two by energetic weekend hikers. Its route up the glaciated Merced River canyon is one of the Sierra's best. Although over half the route lies beyond this guide's area, this popular route is too fine to omit.

Description: See **Day Hike 4** for the first ½ mile east to a stream-gaging station along the east bank of the Merced River. **Day Hike**

Supplementary map: the Merced River Trail. Scale 1:62,000

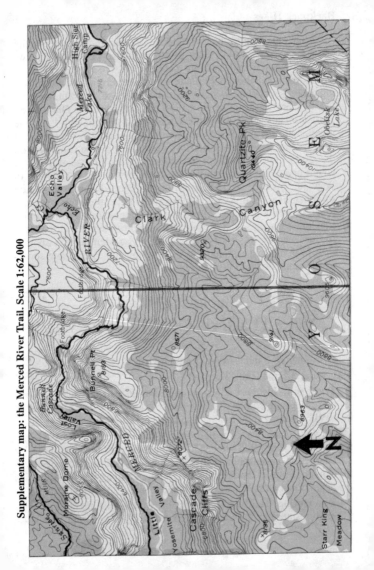

19 describes the route to the Vernal Fall bridge; then you follow the last part of **Day Hike 20** in reverse up the John Muir Trail to Nevada Fall. The last 1¼ miles along this section are very scenic, with views of Half Dome, Mt. Broderick, Liberty Cap, Nevada Fall, and the Merced River canyon. Beyond the Nevada Fall bridge we soon meet the end of the Mist Trail (risky for backpackers), then climb up and over a minor ridge into western Little Yosemite Valley, as described in the first paragraph of **Day Hike 21**.

We leave the northbound John Muir Trail to embark on a shady two-mile stroll, following the Merced Lake Trail through the broad, flat valley. The valley's floor has been largely buried by glacial sediments, which like beach sand make us work even though the trail is level. Progressing east through Little Yosemite Valley, we stay closer to the base of glacier-polished Moraine Dome than to the Merced River, and along this stretch you can branch off to riverside campsites that are far more peaceful than those near the John Muir Trail junction, which tends to be a "Grand Central Station." The valley's east end is graced by the presence of a beautiful pool—the receptacle of a Merced River cascade. Leaving the camps of the picturesque area, we climb past the cascade and glance back to see the east face of exfoliating Moraine Dome.

Our brief cascade climb heads toward the 1,900-foot-high, Bunnell Point cliff, which is exfoliating at a prodigious rate. Rounding the base of a glacier-smoothed dome, unofficially called the Sugar Loaf, we enter shady Lost Valley, in which no fires are allowed. At the valley's east end we switchback up past Bunnell Cascade, which with the magnificent canyon scenery can easily distract us from the real danger of this exposed section of trail. Although the scenery may overpower us, past glaciers, which completely buried Bunnell Point, were powerless to effectively erode this part of the canyon. Just beyond, the canyon floor widens a bit, and in this area we bridge the Merced River. Our up-canyon walk soon reaches a series of more than a dozen switchbacks that carry us up 400 feet above the river—a bypass route necessitated by another gorge. Our climb reaches its zenith amid a spring-fed profuse garden, bordered by aspens, which in midsummer supports a colorful array of various wildflowers.

Merced Lake and a view up-canyon

Beyond this glade we soon come out onto a highly polished bedrock surface. Here we can glance west and see Clouds Rest—a long ridge—standing on the horizon. Now we descend back into tree cover and among the white boles of aspens we brush through a forest carpet of bracken ferns and cross several creeklets before emerging on a bedrock bench above the river's inner gorge. From the bench we can study the features of a broad, hulking granitic mass opposite us whose south face is bounded by an immense arch. A "hairline" crack along its east side indicates that a major rockfall is imminent. Traversing our bench, we soon come to a bend in the river and at it bridge the Merced just above the brink of its cascades. Strolling east, we reach the west end of spacious Echo Valley, and proceed to a junction at its north edge.

Here, near an Echo Creek campsite, is the start of an alternate, less dramatic, high route you could take back to Little Yosemite

Valley. But with Merced Lake our goal, we immediately bridge Echo Creek, strike southeast through boggy Echo Valley, and climb east past the Merced River's largely unseen pools to Merced Lake's west shore. Don't camp here, but rather continue past the north shore to the Merced Lake High Sierra Camp and the adjacent riverside campground, about 9¼ miles beyond the John Muir Trail junction in Little Yosemite Valley. Be sure to use the bearproof storage boxes. Eighty-foot-deep Merced Lake, being a large one at a moderate elevation, supports three species of trout: brook, brown, and rainbow.

Backpack Hike 2
Bridalveil Campground-Wawona Loop

Distance: 30.3 miles (48.7 km) semiloop trip

Grade: 5E, moderate 3-day hike

Trailhead: Bridalveil Campground (see Day Hike 13 trailhead). Park at the campground's *far* end. **C2.**

Introduction: Sparkling lakes, deep canyons, and alpine crests are *not* found along this hike—but then, neither are the backpacking crowds. This is a hike for those who love quiet trails. Although most of it is forested, you will pass through areas that have been burned in lightning-caused forest fires. The trees are regenerating, and until they cast sufficient shade, shrubs and wildflowers will grow in greater abundance.

Description: From the campground's far end, our trail climbs only about 200 feet in the first 3⅓ miles, an excellent way to start a backpack hike. Although white firs and red firs are present, they are greatly overwhelmed by a superabundance of lodgepole pines along this creekside stretch. After about 1.6 miles of it—on a ridge above nearby Bridalveil Creek—we join a trail that comes 1.7 miles from the Glacier Point Road (the **Backpack Hike 3** trailhead). A 1987 fire—one of several in the drainage—caused moderate damage to the forest here. The trail keeps above the creek for a short distance, then curves over to a moderate-size camp along the creek's tributary. Like others we'll meet, this one can have lots of mosquitoes before late July. A two-minute walk upstream from the camp ends at the tributary's ford, and on the east bank we meet our second junction. The lightly used, sometimes obscure trail to the left climbs a short mile east to the Ostrander Lake Trail (**Backpack Hike 3**).

Turning right, we climb gently south for a mile to the tributary's upper basin. In it our climb becomes first moderate, and then steep as we struggle briefly up to a nearby crest that separates the unglaciated Alder Creek drainage from that of the lightly glaciated Bridalveil Creek drainage. Jeffrey pines yield to red firs as we traverse slopes over to a junction near a saddle. The trail we'll return on climbs east to here from Deer Camp.

Starting southeast, we quickly cross the broad saddle, enter the lightly glaciated Chilnualna Creek drainage, and begin a rolling, gentle 1¼-mile descent that goes through several small meadows, all abounding in corn lilies. Just before we reach the next junction, our trail touches the east edge of long Turner Meadows, and here you can make a fair camp.

At the junction we veer right, hop Turner Meadows creek, then our old trail climbs unnecessarily 300 feet up to a ridge (originally, *horses* did the climbing, not hikers, so ups and downs were not an issue). On this moderate, shady ascent one has a crest view of glaciated-but-subdued Buena Vista Peak, to the east. We then start a 3,800-foot drop to the Wawona area. On it western white pines quickly yield to their cousins, the sugar pines, while farther down red firs yield to the closely related white firs. A shrubby black oak appears at about 7,540 feet elevation, near the top of its altitudinal range. This oak is just past a secondary crest, and from it we plunge down to a creeklet, then make an equally long drop to its larger counterpart. From its verdant banks we have an easy ½-mile descent to a junction just above Chilnualna Creek. Here, near the confluence of this creek and its southbound tributary, you can find a suitable spot to spend your first night. You may want to first view Chilnualna Fall, just downstream, but be extremely careful if you do, for the rock can be treacherously slippery and there are no safety railings to keep you from being swept over the fall.

The next day, descend the trail 4.0 scenic miles to its end, following the description of **Day Hike 23** in reverse. Then, gradually descending west, walk 1⅓ miles along a road that goes through the private inholding of North Wawona, which has supplies, food, and lodging. Our next trail, the Alder Creek Trail, begins about ⅓ mile beyond the settlement's school, and this trailhead is about 300 yards before the Wawona District Office, which dispenses information and wilderness permits. Before resuming your loop hike, you might consider a side trip to the Pioneer Yosemite History Center, which you enter just west of a junction with the district office's spur road. By walking 200–300 yards upstream from the center's covered bridge you'll discover some small pools in the South Fork Merced River that in summer afternoons are among the warmest "swimming holes" in the Park.

The Alder Creek Trail begins about 100 yards east of a west-heading service road. At our low elevation temperatures often soar into the 80s by early afternoon, and water may be absent until we reach Alder Creek, about 6 miles ahead. After a brief, initial, open climb north, our trail turns west to make an ascending traverse for ⅓ mile across small gullies. At the end of a 2¾-mile-long, mostly viewless ascent, we reach a mile-high junction, from which a steep trail descends ¾ mile to the heavily traveled Wawona Road.

Starting east, we begin a 2¾-mile rolling traverse in and out of gullies and around or over low ridges to a view of 100-foot-high Alder Creek fall below. Along the last mile or so of this section you may see railroad ties, which are the few tangible relics of a dark period in the Park's history. From the early days of World War I through the 1920s, the Yosemite Lumber Company laid railroad tracks in and around western Park lands to log some of the Sierra's finest stands of sugar pines.

Beyond the fall our abandoned-railroad route approaches lushly lined Alder Creek, parallels it north gently upstream for 1¼ miles, then crosses it to reach a nearby junction. Here or elsewhere along Alder Creek you can make your second night's camp. From the junction a trail climbs north 1⅓ miles to an old logging road, on which you could walk ½ mile east to the trail's resumption, which for a little over 3 miles first climbs and then barely drops on a direct

route to the Bridalveil Campground entrance. Thick brush, however, makes this route undesirable.

The recommended route angles right at the Alder Creek junction, immediately refords the broad creek, and then climbs east for
1¾ miles, paralleling a murmuring tributary. This white-fir-shaded
stretch ends at Deer Camp, a desolate roadend flat along the fringe
of the former logging area. You can camp here, but it lacks esthetics.
Beyond it our trail continues east and, typical of old trails, it winds
and switchbacks all too steeply up most of a 1,100-foot ascent.
Midway up it, views expand, providing us with an overview of the
Alder Creek basin. After about 1¼ miles of climbing, we top a crest,
then momentarily descend to a usually flowing creeklet. Should you
want to camp in this vicinity, do so at the nearby crest top if
mosquitoes are abundant. Leaving the creeklet we climb around a
meadow—rich in sedges, willows, and corn lilies—then make a
final short push southeast up to a junction near a saddle. From it we
retrace our first day's steps 4.9 miles back to the trailhead.

Backpack Hike 3
Glacier Point Road to Ostrander Lake

Distance: 12.7 miles (20.5 km) round trip

Grade: 3C, easy 2-day hike

Trailhead: Branch from the Wawona Road and drive 8.9 miles up
the Glacier Point Road to a turnoff, on your right. This parking area
is 1.3 miles past the Bridalveil Campground spur road. **C2.**

Introduction: Ostrander Lake, being the closest lake to the Glacier
Point Road, is the object of many summertime weekend backpackers. It is also popular in winter and spring with cross-country skiers.

Description: The first half of our hike is easy—a gentle ascent
through a forest that is interspersed with an assortment of meadows.
We start along a former jeep road, and soon encounter the first of
several areas of lodgepole forest badly burned in a 1987 fire. Farther up, on Horizon Ridge, we'll see a forest burned in a 1994 fire.

Note the difference that seven years of regrowth makes. Just ⅓ mile from the trailhead we cross a sluggish creek, then amble an easy mile to a ridge junction. From it a short lateral drops to Bridalveil Creek—possibly a difficult June crossing—then climbs equally briefly to the Bridalveil Creek Trail (**Backpack Hike 2**).

From the junction our route contours southeast past unseen Lost Bear Meadow, and after a mile makes a short ascent east up along a trickling creek to its crossing. Just beyond the ford our road curves west to a nearby junction with a second lateral to the Bridalveil Creek Trail. Though we are now about halfway to Ostrander Lake, we've climbed very little, and from this junction we face 1,500 feet of vertical gain, mostly through burned forests. Nevertheless, some trees survived, and they indicate the former (and future) forest type.

Our steepening road climbs east through a mixed forest, then climbs more gently south across an open slab that provides the first views of the Bridalveil Creek basin. We then curve southeast into a Jeffrey-pine stand, then climb east through a white-fir forest. These firs are largely supplanted by red firs by the time we top a saddle that bisects Horizon Ridge. Climbing southeast up that ridge, our road passes through an open stretch that supports an eastern Sierra species—sagebrush. About 400 feet above our first saddle the road switchbacks at a second one, then curves up to a third. From it our road makes a momentary descent southeast before bending to start a short, final ascent south into unburned forest surrounding Ostrander Lake. Near this bend we get far-ranging views across the Illilouette Creek basin. We can see the tops of Royal Arches and Washington Column and, above and east of them, see North, Basket, and Half domes. Behind Half Dome stands the Park's geographic center, broad-topped Mt. Hoffmann. Reigning over the Illilouette Creek basin is Mt. Starr King and its entourage of lesser domes. To the east and northeast the jagged crest of the Clark Range cuts the sky.

Beyond our short, final ascent south we drop in several minutes to Ostrander Hut. When it is snowbound, cross-country skiers can stay in it, if they've first obtained reservations from the Park's Wilderness Center (see "The Trails," p. 13). The hut is on a rocky glacial moraine left by a glacier that retreated perhaps 15,000 years ago. Behind it, lying in a bedrock basin, is 25-acre, trout-populated Ostrander Lake. Here, camping is good along the west shore.

Experienced hikers can head cross-country southeast ¼ mile to a pond, then east over a ridge to a shallow bowl holding the Hart Lakes. The larger one has a rather stark granitic backdrop, the glacier-smoothed northeast face of Horse Ridge. After perhaps camping nearby, you can then descend northeast to the Buena Vista Trail, hopefully meeting it atop the crest of a sizable moraine. (If you're too low, you may end up at Edson Lake.) Either head down the Buena Vista Trail and then west out the Mono Meadow Trail, for a 19.6-mile (31.6 km) loop trip (with a short vehicle shuttle), or else head up the Buena Vista Trail for more lake hunting, described in the next hike.

Backpack Hike 4
Mono Meadow to Buena Vista and Royal Arch Lakes

Distance: 30.4 miles (48.9 km) round trip

Grade: 5E, easy 4-day hike

Trailhead: Branch from the Wawona Road and drive 10.1 miles up the Glacier Point Road to a forested saddle with a parking area, on your right. **D2.**

Introduction: The subalpine lakes nestled around Buena Vista Peak can be reached from North Wawona—Backpack Hike 5—or from three trailheads along the Glacier Point Road. This hike starts from one of these trailheads and visits five of the area's lakes. Although this route is slightly longer than Backpack Hike 5, it requires 20% less climbing effort.

Description: Shaded by magnificent red firs, our trail begins with a steady, moderate descent north, followed by an easing gradient east to lodgepole-fringed Mono Meadow. Until mid-July you may face 200 yards of muddy freshets and meadow bogs before you reach the narrow meadow's east edge. During this period, desperate hikers try to circumvent the mire, and several paths may spring up to confuse you. The real trail crosses the meadow on a 120° bearing, and it becomes obvious once you're within the forest's edge.

Beyond the meadow our Mono Meadow Trail crosses a low divide, then makes a generally viewless, easy descent to a major tributary of Illilouette Creek. Here, 1½ miles from your trailhead, is your first possible campsite. We ford the tributary at the brink of some rapids, and in early season this ford could be a dangerous one. From the tributary we have a short though unnecessary climb, with 200 feet of elevation gain. The climb does have some merit, for at the crest and on our descent east from it we're rewarded with views of North, Basket, and Half domes, Clouds Rest, and Mt. Starr King. After a descent through a fir forest we emerge on an open slope and descend straight toward Mt. Starr King, the highest of the Illilouette Creek domes.

God bless Yosemite bears!   —John Muir

Immediately after the view disappears, we reach a junction with the Buena Vista Trail, which links Glacier Point with the Buena Vista Peak area. Turning right, we go 40 yards up-canyon to a second junction, from where the Mono Meadow Trail goes 300 yards east past campsites to ford broad Illilouette Creek. From it the trail climbs a slope veneered with glacial outwash—stream deposits from the last glaciers that lay up-canyon—then it crosses a bedrock bench with a veneer of gravel. In the "classic" U.S. Geological Survey Professional Paper 160 on Yosemite Valley, this gravel was considered to be sediments of a hypothetical glacial lake, which supposedly existed hundreds of thousands of years ago. Actually the gravel, as elsewhere in the Sierra, is nothing more than weathered granitic bedrock. This is also true of gravel on benches in this drainage, which incorrectly were called glacial deposits. Of more interest to the hiker is that this spacious bedrock bench is suitable for camping. On it a trail climbs east to a junction near two interesting domes. Two rather mediocre Merced Pass Lakes, lying east beyond our area, by themselves are not worth the 12¾-mile hike from the trailhead to reach them.

From the junction before the creek crossing we climb southeast up the Buena Vista Trail. Over much of our route up toward Buena Vista Peak the vegetation has been burned by several large, natural fires. Usually a burn is quite unsightly for a year or two, but wildflowers often abound in one, and after several years brush and young trees soften the visual effect. In 1¼ miles we come to a creeklet with a fair camp on its west bank. Our trail's gradient gradually eases, then we cross a broad divide and in ¼ mile angle sharply left to descend along the edge of a sloping meadow. Beyond it we encounter aspens that hide a step-across creek. Just a few minutes' walk east of it we cross a slightly larger creek, then make a gentle ascent southeast across sandy soils to steep slopes above Buena Vista Creek. Camping is poor along the west bank, but good—and isolated—above the east bank. Fallen trees may provide access across the bouldery creek to these sites.

Soon our trail leaves Buena Vista Creek, curves southwest and climbs moderately in that direction for 1½ miles to a ford, between two meadows, of diminutive Edson Lake creek. From a poor campsite the trail ascends along a moraine crest, then in one mile leaves it to angle southeast up to a higher crest. Where our trail makes this sudden angle left, you can leave it and contour ⅓ mile west over to a campsite at shallow Edson Lake. Our trail follows the higher moraine crest southwest for more than 300 yards, finally leaves the burned area, and then makes a ¼-mile, view-packed descent to Hart Lakes creek. From where the trail leaves the crest, you can continue cross-country southwest up it, soon diagonal up slabs, then climb south up to the Hart Lakes.

From brush-lined Hart Lakes creek we make a short contour over to Buena Vista Creek, having a small campsite on its east bank. After ½ mile of moderate ascent we cross a creek that bends northeast, then continue south up a slightly shorter ascent to a recrossing of that creek. Immediately beyond we cross its western tributary, then follow this stream south briefly up to two ponds, from which we switchback up a cirque wall with ice-shattered blocks to a crest junction. **Backpack Hike 5**, ascending from North Wawona, now joins our route for a loop around the lakes of Buena Vista Peak. The first lake we encounter, about ⅓ mile southeast from the junction, is

Horse Ridge stands above the larger Hart Lake

rather bleak Buena Vista Lake, which has rainbow and brook trout. Nestled on a broad bench at the base of the cool north slope of Buena Vista Peak, this lake is the highest and coldest one we'll see. It does, however, have two good camps.

Starting at the lake's outlet, we ascend short switchbacks up to a broad pass. From the viewless pass you can climb ¾ mile up a gentle ridge to Buena Vista Peak for an unrestricted panorama of the Park's southern area. From the pass we descend two easy, winding trail miles to a favorite lake on this loop, Royal Arch Lake, which lies below a broad, granitic arch. This lake, like Buena Vista Lake, has rainbow and brook trout. Just past the outlet, near the lake's southwest corner, is an excellent, though often occupied, campsite. For more solitude you can head cross-country ¾ mile west to less attractive Minnow Lake, which has brook trout.

Leaving Royal Arch Lake, we parallel its outlet creek for ½ mile, then angle south across slabs to a junction with a trail that goes first to Buck Camp (a ranger station) and then to Chiquito Pass. From the junction we descend west toward Johnson Lake, reaching good campsites along its northwest shore in just ¾ mile—with hordes of mosquitoes in early season. We don't see large Crescent Lake, but on meeting its inlet creek, about ⅓ mile beyond a meadowy divide, one can walk 150 yards downstream, passing a fair camp before reaching the lake's shallow, trout-filled waters. You might visit or camp near the lake's south end, for from its outlet you can peer into the 2,800-foot-deep South Fork Merced River canyon.

Beyond Crescent Lake's inlet creek our trail quickly turns north, passes a small creekside meadow, and then climbs more than 150 feet to a second broad divide. From it we descend into the headwaters of a Chilnualna Creek tributary. Our moderate-to-steep gradient ends when we approach easily missed Grouse Lake. Look for a use trail that descends about 100 yards to a fair campsite on the north shore of this shallow, reedy lakelet.

Lodgepoles and red firs monopolize the slopes along our two-mile descent from this lake down to a hillside junction. From here, hikers completing **Backpack Hike 5** head west down-canyon to their trailhead. Hikers on the second day of that hike join us for a short northwest stretch, first up over a nearby divide, then down more than 400 feet to Chilnualna Creek. Just above its north bank is

Royal Arch Lake is well-named

a good, medium-size campsite, and just beyond that is another trail junction. From it **Backpack Hike 5** trekkers climb east. Should you want to visit the Chilnualna Lakes, take this 5.3-mile trail up past them to the crest junction where **Backpack Hike 5** first joined our route, then backtrack 13.1 miles to your trailhead. This route is 10.0 miles longer than the following route, including its 1.2-mile walk along the Glacier Point Road back to the trailhead.

Spurning the longer option, we head northwest from Chilnualna Creek. During midsummer, our gently ascending traverse is brightened by the orange sunbursts of alpine lilies, growing chest-high along the wetter parts of our trail. As we near Turner Meadows we encounter a trail junction from which **Backpack Hike 2** departs southwest down to the Wawona area.

We now backtrack along the first part of that hike, first ascending past and through a series of "Turner Meadows," then topping a forest pass to quickly meet a trail descending to Deer Camp. We, however, keep right, traverse to a crest and descend to a tributary of Bridalveil Creek. But before reaching Bridalveil Creek, we meet a junction, turn left and then cross the tributary creek. Along it we momentarily pass a moderate-size campsite and then in ½ mile reach another junction. The main trail continues 1.6 miles northwest to Bridalveil Campground, but we veer right, drop to nearby Bridalveil Creek, ford it, and make an equally short climb up to the Ostrander Lake Trail—a closed jeep road. In 1½ miles our northbound route ends at the Glacier Point Road, beside which we walk 1.2 miles east to our trailhead.

Backpack Hike 5
North Wawona to Royal Arch, Buena Vista, and Chilnualna Lakes

Distance: 28.3 miles (45.6 km) semiloop trip
Grade: 5E, easy 4-day hike
Trailhead: Same as the Day Hike 23 trailhead. **C5.**

Introduction: Glaciers originating on the slopes of Buena Vista Peak descended north, south, and west, then retreated to leave about a dozen small-to-medium-size lakes. This hike visits seven of these plus dashing Chilnualna Fall—one of the Park's highest falls outside Yosemite Valley.

Description: Day Hike 23 guides you up through a changing forest to campsites—a possible first night's stop—in an area around a trail junction near a south-flowing tributary of Chilnualna Creek. From that tributary our trail makes a short, steep ascent northeast, then traverses southeast. Soon reaching Chilnualna Creek, you'll find additional campsites along both its banks.

After crossing to the southeast bank, we head upstream, then veer away from the creek to make a short, moderate ascent to a low gap. Past it we enter a damp meadow—an early-season mosquito haven—then climb for a mile, paralleling the usually unseen creek at a distance before we intersect its tributary, Grouse Lake creek. Generally a jump-across creek, it can be a 20-foot wide, slippery-slab ford in June. Now just above 7,000 feet, we feel the effects of a higher elevation as well as see them—as expressed in the predominance of stately red firs and occasional lodgepole pines. Before reaching a junction after a ¾-mile ascent, we also note our first trailside western white pines.

At the junction we join **Backpack Hike 4** for a short northwest stretch, first up over a nearby divide, then down more than 400 feet to Chilnualna Creek. Just above its north bank is a good, medium-size campsite, and just beyond that is another trail junction. Here we turn right while **Backpack Hike 4** continues ahead, bound for Turner Meadows and the Glacier Point Road.

Eastbound, we make a moderate ¼-mile ascent, followed by a gentler one that goes 1¼ miles along the lodgepole-shaded bank of Chilnualna Creek. After a ¼-mile walk along this gentler stretch, you'll find an acceptable campsite. At the end of the stretch we cross the seasonal creek that drains the middle and northern Chilnualna Lakes. We go a few yards along the larger creek that drains the southern and eastern Chilnualna Lakes, then leave it to cross a nearby bouldery ridge of a glacial moraine.

Young glacial evidence in the form of moraines, erratics, and polish is often seen along the remaining 1⅔-mile, shady climb to the waist-deep southern Chilnualna Lake. Being so shallow, it is one this route's warmest lakes for cooling off in. The best of the Chilnualna Lakes is also the least visited: the lake at the base of Buena Vista Peak's western shoulder, about ½ mile east-southeast of our trailside lake. A more-frequented lake is the middle one, which is easier to reach. From the far end of our lake, head ¼ mile up its inlet creek to a small pond, then walk due north over a low ridge to the middle lake. From it one can easily regain the trail by continuing north—no need to drop along its outlet creek.

Leaving the trailside lake and its fair west-shore campsite, we climb over a low, bouldery morainal ridge, skirt a small meadow, and cross the middle lake's ephemeral creek. Past it we curve clockwise over to the northern lake's outlet creek, parallel it upward, and then, just ¼ mile before the lake, cross over to the north bank. Upon reaching the shallow, narrow lake we find a good campsite among red firs and western white pines. If weather is threatening, camp here rather than climb east to the exposed pass.

At that 9,040-foot-high pass, about a ¾-mile winding ascent from the northern lake, we meet the Buena Vista Trail. Now we follow most of the second half of **Backpack Hike 4** as it goes past Buena Vista, Royal Arch, Johnson, Crescent, and Grouse lakes. You may want to visit all of them, and you should plan to spend at least a day in this scenic glacier-lake area. A little more than two miles west of Grouse Lake you'll leave **Backpack Hike 4** where you first met it, and descend the way you came—past Chilnualna Fall.

Recommended Reading

Arce, Gary. 1995. *Defying Gravity: High Adventure on Yosemite's Walls.* Berkeley: Wilderness Press, 194 p.

Aune, Philip S., technical coordinator. 1994. *Proceedings of the Symposium on Giant Sequoias: Their Place in the Ecosystem and Society.* Albany, CA: U.S. Forest Service Pacific Southwest Research Station, 170 p.

Calkins, Frank C., N. King Huber, and Julie A. Roller. 1985. *Bedrock geologic map of Yosemite Valley, Yosemite National Park, California.* Washington: U.S. Geological Survey, Map I-1639.

Gaines, David. 1988. *Birds of Yosemite and the East Slope.* Lee Vining, CA: Artemisia Press, 352 p.

Gibbens, Robert P., and Harold F. Heady. 1964. *The Influence of Modern Man on the Vegetation of Yosemite Valley.* Berkeley: Univ. of Calif. Div. of Agricultural Sciences, Manual 36, 44 p.

Grater, Russell K., and Tom A. Blaue. 1978. *Discovering Sierra Mammals.* El Portal, CA: Yosemite Association, 174 p.

Hickman, James C., editor. 1993. *The Jepson Manual: Higher Plants of California.* Berkeley: University of California Press, 1400 p.

Huber, N. King. 1987. *The Geologic Story of Yosemite National Park.* Washington: U.S. Geological Survey, Bulletin 1595. 68 p.

Huber, N. King, Paul C. Bateman, and Clyde Wahrhaftig. 1989. *Geologic Map of Yosemite National Park and Vicinity, California.* Washington: U.S. Geological Survey, Map I-1874.

Niehaus, Theodore F., and Charles L. Ripper. 1976. *A Field Guide to Pacific States Wildflowers.* Boston: Houghton Mifflin Company, 432 p.

Reid, Don. 1993. *Yosemite Climbs: Big Walls.* Evergreen, CO: Chockstone Press, 211 p.

Reid, Don. 1994. *Yosemite Climbs: Free Climbs.* Evergreen, CO: Chockstone Press, 413 p.

Russell, Carl P. 1992. *One hundred years in Yosemite.* El Portal, CA: Yosemite Association, 269 p.

Schaffer, Jeffrey P. 1992. *Yosemite National Park: A Natural-History Guide to Yosemite and Its Trails.* Berkeley: Wilderness Press, 274 p.

Schaffer, Jeffrey P. 1995. *The Geomorphic Evolution of the Sierra Nevada, east-central California, with emphasis on Yosemite Valley* [Ph.D. thesis: third, *unabridged* draft]. Berkeley, University of California.

Schaffer, Jeffrey P. 1996. *Riddles in the Rocks: Solving the Enigmatic Origin of Yosemite Valley and the Sierra Nevada.* Berkeley: Wilderness Press, 192 p.

Stebbins, Robert C. 1972. *Amphibians and Reptiles of California.* Berkeley: Univ. of Calif. Press, 152 p.

Whitney, Stephen. 1979. *A Sierra Club Naturalist's Guide to the Sierra Nevada.* San Francisco: Sierra Club Books, 526 p.

Willard, Dwight. 1995. *Giant Sequoia Groves of the Sierra Nevada: a Reference Guide.* Self-published: Box 7304, Berkeley, CA 94707, 361 p.

Index